10

MINUTE GUIDE TO

MICROSOFT®
WORD 97

by Peter Aitken

A Division of Macmillan Computer Publishing
201 W. 103rd Street, Indianapolis, Indiana 46290 USA

©1996 by Que® Corporation

Library of Congress Catalog Card Number: 96-70780

International Standard Book Number: 07897-1019-6

98 97 96   8 7 6 5 4 3 2 1

Interpretation of the printing code: the rightmost double-digit number is the year of the book's first printing; the rightmost single-digit number is the number of the book's printing. For example, a printing code of 96-1 shows that this copy of the book was printed during the first printing of the book in 1996.

Printed in the United States of America

Publisher Roland Elgey

Vice President and Publisher Marie Butler-Knight

Publishing Manager Lynn E. Zingraf

Editorial Services Director Elizabeth Keaffaber

Managing Editor Michael Cunningham

Acquisitions Editor Martha O'Sullivan

Technical Specialist Richard F. Brown

Product Development Specialist Faithe Wempen

Product Editor Theresa Mathias

Book Designer Barbara Kordesh

Cover Designer Dan Armstrong

Production Team Trina Brown, Angela Calvert, Lori Cliburn, William Huys Jr., Beth Rago, and Laure Robinson

Indexer Nadia Ibrahim

CONTENTS

INTRODUCTION

Welcome to Microsoft Word 97. The latest release of Microsoft's flag-ship word processing program brings even more power and features to a program that was already considered to be the best of its type. No matter what kind of document you need to create—a simple memo, a World Wide Web page, or a 500-page re-port—Word can handle it, and make you look good in the process!

Word is surprisingly easy to use, but any program with so much power cannot avoid being somewhat complex. How do you go about learning the ins and outs of Word so you can start using it to get something done? You could go to a bookstore and buy one of those 1,200-page books that covers every single part of Word in excruciat-ing detail—but do you have time to read a 1,200-page book? What you need is a quick way to learn the important parts of Word, those parts of the program that you'll need most often in your day-to-day word processing tasks. Let me say modestly that you have chosen exactly the right book!

The 10 Minute Guide to Word 97 is designed for people just like you. In these pages, you will learn the basics of Word in a series of short, easy-to-understand lessons. Each lesson is self-contained and can be completed in 10 minutes or less, permitting you to start and stop as your schedule allows. There's no padding in this book—it's loaded with clear, concise information that you really use.

WHAT IS THE 10 MINUTE GUIDE?

The *10 Minute Guide* series takes a different approach to teaching people how to use a computer program. We do not attempt to cover every detail of the program. Instead, each book concentrates on the program features that are essential for most users, the features that you need to get your work done. Our goal is to teach you, as quickly and painlessly as possible, those things you need to start using the program for productive, real-world work.

USING THIS BOOK

The 10 Minute Guide to Word 97 contains a total of 32 lessons. Ideally, you should work through them in order. After reading the first five lessons, however, you can skip around to find specific information as quickly as possible. When you complete the book, you should have a good knowledge of the most important parts of Word, and should be able to complete almost all word processing tasks with ease.

Several special elements are used throughout the book to highlight specific types of information.

Timesaver Tip   These are helpful suggestions to get you working more efficiently.

Plain English   Non-technical definitions of terms that may be unfamiliar to some readers.

Panic Button   Warning of possible problems, and information on how to solve them.

Several other of the book's features are designed to make your learning faster and easier:

➤ Numbered steps provide exact instructions for commonly needed procedures.

➤ Menu commands, toolbar buttons, and dialog box options that you select are printed in blue for easy recognition.

➤ Text that you enter is **boldface and blue**.

➤ Messages that appear on-screen are **boldface**.

ACKNOWLEDGMENTS

While this book has but a single author, it is in many ways a team effort. Faithe Wempen, Product Development Specialist, and Theresa Mathias, Production Editor, were instrumental in converting my rough chapters into a finished product. Rick Brown, Technical Specialist, made sure that no technical errors slipped through. Thanks, everyone.

THE AUTHOR

Peter Aitken is a widely read computer book author, with more than two dozen books to his credit, including *10 Minute Guide to Lotus 1-2-3*. He lives in Chapel Hill, North Carolina, and is employed at Duke University Medical Center.

TRADEMARKS

All terms mentioned in this book that are known to be trademarks have been appropriately capitalized. Que cannot attest to the accuracy of this information. Use of a term in this book should not be regarded as affecting the validity of any trademark or service mark.

GETTING STARTED WITH WORD

In this lesson, you learn how to start and exit Word and to identify the parts of the Word screen. You also learn the basics of entering text.

STARTING WORD FOR WINDOWS

You start Word from the Windows Start menu. Follow these steps:

1. Open the Start menu by clicking the Start button.

2. On the Start menu, click Programs.

3. On the next menu, click Microsoft Word.

Another way to start Word is to open the Start menu and click New Office Document. Or, if the Office Shortcut Bar is displayed along the right edge of your screen, click the New Office Document button. Either way, the New dialog box appears. In this dialog box, click the General tab (if necessary) then double-click the Blank Document icon.

Can't find Microsoft Word on the menu? You must install Word (or Office) on your system before you can use it. Please refer to the inside front cover for instructions.

UNDERSTANDING THE WORD SCREEN

When you start Word, you see a blank document ready for you to enter text. Before you begin, however, you need to know about the various parts of the screen (see Figure 1.1). You'll use these screen elements, which are described in Table 1.1, as you work on your documents.

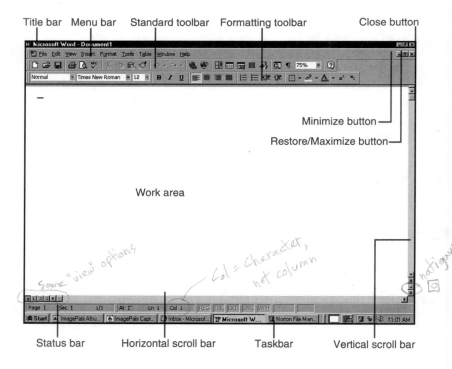

FIGURE 1.1   Parts of the Word screen.

TABLE 1.1   PARTS OF THE WORD SCREEN

SCREEN ELEMENT	FUNCTION
Work area	Your document displays here for text entry and editing. Figure 1.1 shows a blank document.
Title bar	The program name, user name, and the name of the current document display here. At the right end of the title bar are buttons to minimize, restore, and close the program.

SCREEN ELEMENT	FUNCTION
Menu bar	Menu headings on this bar let you access Word's menu commands.
Toolbars	The small pictures, or *buttons*, on the toolbars let you select commonly needed commands by clicking the mouse.
Status bar	Word displays information about the document and the state of the keyboard lock keys on the Status bar.
Scroll bars	You click on the scroll bars to move around in your document.
Minimize button	Click this button to temporarily hide Word. Then, click the Microsoft Word button on the taskbar at the bottom of your screen to re-display Word.
Close button	Click this button to close Word.
Restore/Maximize button	Click this button to enlarge Word to full-screen or to shrink Word to a partial-screen window.

USING MENUS AND TOOLBARS

As you use Word, you will issue commands to tell Word what actions you want done. You can carry out most Word commands using either the menus or the toolbars. The method you use depends on your personal preference.

To select a menu command:

1. Open a menu by clicking the menu title on the menu bar. You can also open a menu by holding down the Alt key then pressing the underlined letter in the menu title. For example, press Alt+F (hold down Alt and press F) to open the File menu.

2. On the open menu, click the desired command or press the underlined letter of the command name.

Throughout this book, I will use a shorthand to specify menu commands. For example, if I say click File, Open, it means to open the File menu then select the Open command.

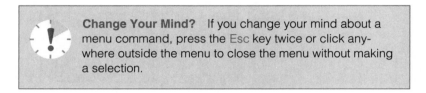

Change Your Mind? If you change your mind about a menu command, press the Esc key twice or click anywhere outside the menu to close the menu without making a selection.

Figure 1.2 shows the open File menu. There are several elements that Word uses on its menus to provide you with additional information. Table 1.2 explains these elements.

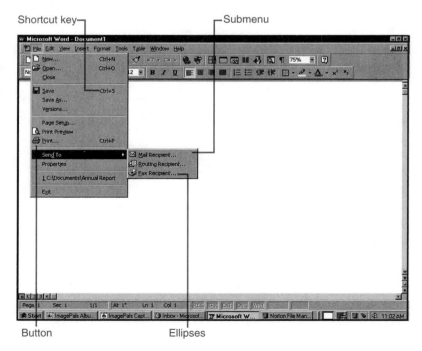

FIGURE 1.2   The File menu with the Send To submenu displayed.

TABLE 1.2   PARTS OF A MENU

MENU ELEMENT	FUNCTION
Button	If the menu command has a corresponding toolbar button, the button is displayed next to the menu command.
Ellipses (...)	Indicates that the menu command leads to a dialog box.
Submenu arrow	Indicates that the menu command leads to another menu (called a submenu).
Shortcut key	Identifies the keys you can use to select the menu command using the keyboard.

You can use shortcut keys to select some commands without using the menus at all. Shortcuts keys are listed on the menu next to the corresponding command. In Figure 1.2, for example, you can see that the shortcut key for the Open command is Ctrl+O. This means that pressing Ctrl+O (press and hold the Ctrl key, press the O key, then release both keys) has the same effect as clicking File, Open.

To use the toolbars, simply use your mouse to click on the desired button. The buttons have pictures on them to help you identify each button's function. You can jog your memory by resting the mouse cursor on a button for a few seconds without clicking. Word will display a *Tooltip* identifying its function next to the button.

 What's This?   Press Shift+F1 to activate What's This help. Then click on any element on the Word screen to view information about it.

WORKING IN DIALOG BOXES

Many of Word's commands result in a *dialog box*. Word uses dialog boxes to obtain additional information required to carry out a command. Each dialog box is different, but they all use the same basic elements.

In a dialog box, press the Tab key to move from item to item; press Shift+Tab to move backwards. You can click an item or press Alt plus the underlined letter to select an item. When the dialog box selections are complete, press Enter or click the OK button to accept your entries and carry out the command. Click the Cancel button or press Esc to close the dialog box without carrying out the command.

ENTERING TEXT AND MOVING AROUND

Word displays a blinking vertical line in the work area. This is the *cursor* or *insertion point,* and it identifies the location in the document where text will be inserted and where certain editing actions will occur. To enter text, simply type it on the keyboard. You should not press Enter at the end of a line—Word will automatically wrap the text to a new line when you reach the right margin. Press Enter only when you want to start a new paragraph.

If you make a mistake, there are a couple of ways you can delete it:

- Press the Backspace key to erase characters to the left of the cursor.

- Press the Delete key to erase characters to the right of the cursor.

You can move the cursor around to add and edit text in different document locations. Table 1.3 describes the basic cursor movements.

TABLE **1.3** MOVING THE CURSOR

TO MOVE THE CURSOR...	DO THIS
To any visible location	Click the location with the mouse
One character right or left	Press the left or right arrow key
One line up or down	Press the up or down arrow key
To the start or end of the line	Press the Home or End key
To the start or end of the document	Hold the Ctrl key and press Home or End

You'll learn more about moving around Word in Lesson 3.

QUITTING THE PROGRAM

When you are finished working with Word, you have several options for exiting the program. All of these methods have the same result:

- Click File, Exit.
- Press Alt+F4.
- Click the Close button on the title bar.

If you have an unsaved document, Word will prompt you to save it before exiting. For now, you can just select No. You'll learn about saving documents in Lesson 4.

In this lesson, you learned how to start and exit Word, how to use menus and toolbars, and you learned about the basics of entering and editing text. The next lesson shows you how to create a new Word document.

CREATING A NEW DOCUMENT

In this lesson, you learn how to create a new Word document and about the relationship between documents and templates. You also learn how to use Wizards.

UNDERSTANDING DOCUMENT TEMPLATES

To work effectively with Word, you must understand that every Word document is based on a *template*. As the name suggests, a template is a model for a document.

Some templates contain no text, giving you a blank document with some basic formatting specifications in which you are responsible for entering all of the text. Other templates contain text and/or detailed formatting specifications. For example, if you write a lot of business letters, you could use a template that contains the date, your return address, and a closing salutation. When you create a new document based on that template, all of those elements will automatically be in the document—all you need to do is add the other parts. If a template contains formatting, then all documents based on that template will have a uniform appearance (for example, the same font and margins).

Word comes with a variety of predefined templates that are ready for you to use. These templates cover a range of common document needs, such as fax forms, memos, business letters, and Web pages. You can also create your own templates. In this lesson, you learn how to use Word's predefined templates. Lesson 17 shows you how to create your own templates.

Document Template A model for a new document that may contain text and/or formatting.

STARTING A NEW DOCUMENT

Many of the documents you create will be based on the Normal template, which creates a blank document. As you learned in Lesson 1, when you start Word it automatically opens a blank document for you to work with. If Word is already running, you can create a blank document by clicking the New button on the toolbar.

To start a document based on another, non-blank template, follow these steps:

1. Click File, New. The New dialog box appears.

2. The tabs along the top of the dialog box list the different template categories. Click the tab corresponding to the category of document you want to create.

3. Click the icon that corresponds to the template you want. If a preview of the template's appearance is available, it will appear in the Preview area. Figure 2.1 shows a preview of the Professional Resume template.

4. Click OK. Word creates the document and displays it, ready for editing.

When you create a document based on a template, the template's text and formatting will be displayed in the new document. There's nothing special about document text that came from a template—you can edit it just like any other text. You can also edit the actual templates, as you'll learn in Lesson 17.

A Wizard icon

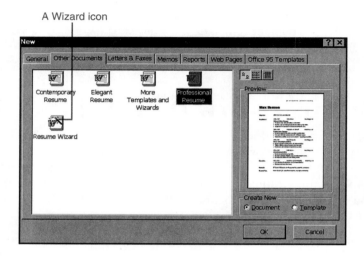

FIGURE 2.1   The New dialog box.

 TIP   **Word on the Web: Web Templates**   Select the Web Pages tab in the New dialog box for templates that are useful for Web documents.

Some templates contain placeholder text that you must replace. For example, the resumé template contains a dummy name and biography that you must delete and replace with your own information. For example, the document might display **[Click here and type your name]**. Simply follow the instructions displayed in brackets.

    No Templates?   If you can't find any templates, they probably were not installed with Word. You can re-install Word, choosing the Custom Setup installation option and specifying which templates you want installed.

USING WIZARDS

Some of Word's templates are a special kind of template called a *Wizard*. Whereas a standard template is a static combination of text and formatting, a Wizard is an active tool that asks you questions about the document you want to create, and then uses your answers to create the new document. When you're starting a new document, you can recognize a Wizard in the New dialog box by its title and the small "magic wand" in its icon. You can see a Wizard template icon in Figure 2.1.

Each Wizard is unique, but they all follow the same basic procedures. There are a number of steps in a Wizard; each step asks you for certain information about the document you want to create. Figure 2.2 shows an example; this is a step in the Fax Wizard. Table 2.1 describes the different components of the Wizard dialog box.

TABLE 2.1   PARTS OF A WIZARD DIALOG BOX

WIZARD COMPONENT	FUNCTION
Title bar	Shows the name of the Wizard that is running.
Flow diagram	Graphically represents the Wizard steps, with the current step highlighted. Click any step to go directly to it.
Information area	Requests document information from you.
Cancel button	Cancels the Wizard without creating a new document.
Back button	Moves to the previous Wizard step.
Next Button	Moves to the next Wizard step.
Finish button	Ends the Wizard and creates the new document based on the information you have entered so far.

continues

TABLE 2.1 CONTINUED

WIZARD COMPONENT	FUNCTION
Help button	Click to display Help information about using the Wizard.

Flow diagram   Information area

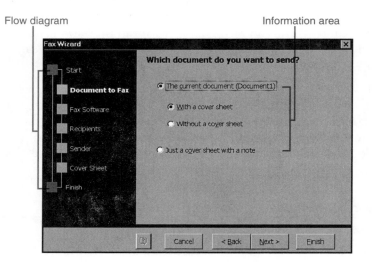

FIGURE 2.2   The Fax Wizard dialog box.

To create a new document using a Wizard, follow these steps:

1. Click File, New to open the New dialog box (refer to Figure 2.1).

2. Click the tab corresponding to the category of document you are creating. Not all tabs contain Wizards, however.

3. Click the icon of the Wizard you want to use, then select OK.

4. In the Wizard dialog box, enter the information needed based on how you want the document created, then click Next.

5. Repeat step 4 for each of the Wizard steps. If needed, click Back one or more times to return to an earlier step to make changes in the information.

6. At the last Wizard step, click Finish to close the Wizard and create the new document.

 TIP **Know Your Templates** Spend some time becoming familiar with Word's various predefined templates—they can save you a lot of time.

In this lesson, you learned about document templates and how to create a new document. You also learned how to use Wizards. The next lesson teaches you how to perform basic editing tasks in Word.

BASIC EDITING TASKS

3

In this lesson, you learn how to enter text, move around in a document, and perform other basic editing tasks.

ENTERING TEXT

When you start a new Word document based on the Normal template, you see a blank work area that contains only two items:

- Blinking vertical line. This is the cursor, or insertion point, and marks the location where text you type appears in the document and where certain editing actions occur.

- Horizontal line. This marks the end of the document.

In a new, empty document these two markers are at the same location. To enter text, simply type it using the keyboard. As you type, the text appears and the insertion point moves to the right. If the line of text reaches the right edge of the screen, Word automatically starts a new line; this is called *word wrapping*. Do not press Enter unless you want to start a new paragraph. As you enter more lines than will fit on the screen, Word scrolls previously entered text upward to keep the cursor in view. Figure 3.1 illustrates word wrap as well as the end of document marker and cursor.

TIP **Leave It to Word Wrap** Press Enter only when you want to start a new paragraph.

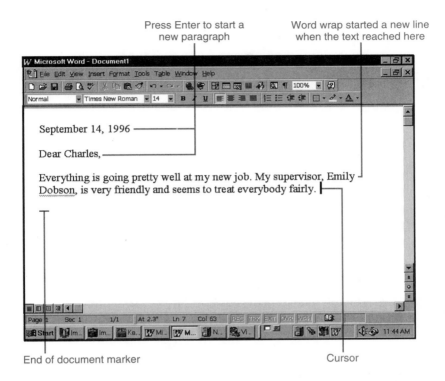

Press Enter to start a new paragraph

Word wrap started a new line when the text reached here

End of document marker

Cursor

FIGURE 3.1 Using Enter and word wrap.

PARAGRAPHS IN WORD

The idea of paragraphs is important in Word because certain types of formatting apply to individual paragraphs. In Word, you end one paragraph and start a new one by pressing Enter. Word inserts a new, blank line and positions the cursor at the beginning of it.

¶ On your screen, the result may look the same as if word wrap had started the new line, but the difference is that Word has inserted a *paragraph mark*. These marks are normally invisible, but you can display them by clicking the Show/Hide ¶ button on the Standard toolbar. Click the button again to hide the marks. This tool is very useful when you need to see exactly where the paragraphs begin and end in your document.

Other Marks? When you display paragraph marks, Word also displays spaces as dots and tabs as arrows.

To combine two paragraphs into a single paragraph, follow these steps:

1. Move the cursor to the beginning of the first line of the second paragraph.
2. Press the Backspace key to delete the paragraph mark.

MOVING AROUND THE DOCUMENT

As you work on a document, you will often have to move the cursor to view or work on other parts of the text. Most of the time you'll use the keyboard, as explained in Table 3.1.

TABLE 3.1   MOVING THE CURSOR WITH THE KEYBOARD

TO MOVE...	PERFORM THIS ACTION
Left or right one character	Press ⇐ or ⇒
Left or right one word	Press Ctrl+⇐ or Ctrl+⇒
Up or down one line	Press ⇑ or ⇓
Up or down one paragraph	Press Ctrl+⇑ or Ctrl+⇓
To the start or end of a line	Press Home or End
Up or down one screen	Press Page Up or Page Down
To the top or bottom of the current screen	Press Ctrl+Page Up or Ctrl+Page Down
To the start or end of the document	Press Ctrl+Home or Ctrl+End

You can also navigate with the mouse. If the desired cursor location is in view on the screen, simply click on the location. If the desired location is not in view, you must scroll to bring it into view and then click on the location. Table 3.2 describes how to scroll with the mouse.

TABLE 3.2   SCROLLING WITH THE MOUSE

TO SCROLL...	DO THIS
Up or down one line	Click the up or down arrow on the vertical scroll bar.
Up or down one screen	Click the vertical toolbars scroll bar between the box and the up or down arrow.
Up or down any amount	Drag the scroll bar box up or down.
Up or down one page	Click the Previous Page or Next Page button on the vertical scroll bar.

Note that scrolling with the mouse does not move the cursor; the cursor remains in its original location while the screen displays another part of the document. You must click the new location to move the cursor there.

TIP   **Quick Go To**   Press Shift+F5 one or more times to move the cursor to locations in the document that you edited most recently.

SELECTING TEXT

Many tasks you'll perform in Word will require that you first select the text you want to modify. For example, to underline a sentence, you must select the sentence first and then click the Underline button. Selected text appears on the screen in reverse video, as shown in Figure 3.2, which has the phrase **Dear Ms. Kennedy:** selected.

Selected text

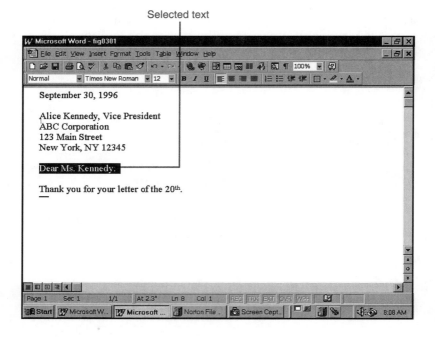

FIGURE 3.2   Selected text appears in reverse video.

You can select text with either the mouse or the keyboard. With the mouse, you can use the selection bar, an unmarked column in the left document margin. When the mouse pointer moves from the document to the selection bar, it changes from an I-beam to an arrow pointing up and to the right. Table 3.3 lists the methods you can use to select text.

TABLE 3.3   METHODS OF SELECTING TEXT

TO SELECT TEXT	PERFORM THIS ACTION
With the mouse	
Any amount	Point at the start of the text, press and hold the left mouse button, and drag the highlight over the text.

To select text	Perform this action
With the mouse	
One word	Double-click anywhere on the word.
One sentence	Press and hold Ctrl and click anywhere in the sentence.
One line	Click the selection bar next to the line.
Multiple lines	Drag in the selection bar next to the lines.
One paragraph	Double-click the selection bar next to the paragraph.
Entire document	Press and hold Ctrl and click anywhere in the selection bar.
With the keyboard	
Any amount	Move the insertion point to the start of the text, press and hold Shift, and move the insertion point to the end of the desired text using the movement keys described in Table 3.1.
Entire document	Press Ctrl+A.

To cancel a selection, click anywhere on the screen or use the keyboard to move the insertion point.

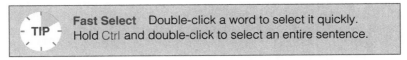

TIP   **Fast Select**   Double-click a word to select it quickly. Hold Ctrl and double-click to select an entire sentence.

When you are selecting text by dragging with the mouse, Word's default is to automatically select entire words. If you need to select partial words, you can turn this option off (or back on) as follows:

1. Click Tools, Options to open the Options dialog box.

2. Click the Edit tab.

3. Click the When Selecting, Automatically Select Entire Word check box to turn it on or off.

4. Click OK.

DELETING, COPYING, AND PASTING TEXT

You have already learned how to use the Delete and Backspace keys to delete single characters. You can delete larger amounts of text, and you can move or copy text from one document location to another.

To delete a block of text, first select the text, then:

- To simply delete the text, press Delete or Backspace.

- To delete the text and replace it with new text, type the new text.

To move or copy text, start by selecting the text, then:

1. To copy the text, click Edit, Copy; click the Copy button on the Standard toolbar; or press Ctrl+C.

   Or, to move the text, click Edit, Cut; click the Cut button on the Standard toolbar; or press Ctrl+X.

2. Move the cursor to the location where you want the text moved or copied.

3. Click Edit, Paste; click the Paste button on the Standard toolbar; or press Ctrl+V.

You can also use the mouse to move and copy text. This technique is most convenient for small amounts of text and when the "from" and "to" locations are both visible on-screen. Here's how:

1. Select the text.

2. Point at the text with the mouse. The mouse pointer changes from an I-beam to an arrow.

3. To copy the text, press and hold Ctrl. To move the text, do not press any key.

4. Drag to the new location. As you drag, a vertical dotted line indicates the text's new location.

5. Release the mouse button and, if you are copying, the Ctrl key.

 Make a Mistake?   You can recover from most editing actions, such as deleting text, by clicking Edit, Undo or by pressing Ctrl+Z.

In this lesson, you learned how to enter text, move around the document, and perform other basic editing tasks. In the next lesson, you'll learn how to save and retrieve documents.

SAVING AND OPENING DOCUMENTS

In this lesson, you learn how to name your document, save it to disk, and enter summary information. You also learn how to open a document you saved earlier.

SAVING A NEW DOCUMENT

When you create a new document in Word, it is stored temporarily in your computer's memory under the default name Document$n$, where n is a number that increases by 1 for each new unnamed document. The document is only "remembered" until you quit the program or turn off the computer. To save a document permanently so you can retrieve it later, you must assign a name and save it to disk.

1. Click File, Save; click the Save button on the Standard toolbar; or press Ctrl+S. The Save As dialog box appears (see Figure 4.1).

2. In the File Name text box, enter the name you want to assign to the document file. The name can be up to 256 characters long and should be descriptive of the document contents.

3. If you want to save the document in a different folder or drive, click the Save In drop-down arrow and select a different folder and/or drive.

4. Click Save. The document is saved to disk and the name you assigned appears in the title bar.

Save In list box   File Name text box

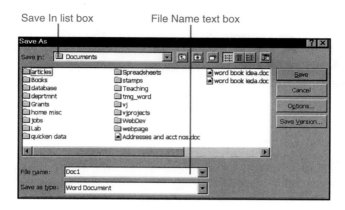

FIGURE 4.1   The Save As dialog box.

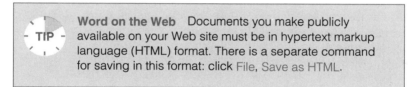

Word on the Web   Documents you make publicly
available on your Web site must be in hypertext markup
language (HTML) format. There is a separate command
for saving in this format: click File, Save as HTML.

SAVING A DOCUMENT AS YOU WORK

After naming and saving a document, you still need to save it
periodically as you work to minimize data loss in the event of a
power failure or other system problem. After you name a
document, you can easily save the current version:

- Click File, Save.
- Click the Save button on the Standard toolbar.
- Press Ctrl+S.

Word automatically uses the document's current name, and no
dialog boxes appear.

Don't Forget! Save your document regularly as you work on it. Otherwise you may loose your work if there is a power outage or other problem.

CHANGING A DOCUMENT'S NAME

After you name a document, you may need to change its name. For example, you can keep an old version of a document under its original name and save a revised version under a new name. To change a document name, follow these steps:

1. Click File, Save As. The Save As dialog box appears, and shows the current document name in the File Name text box.

2. In the File Name text box, change the file name to the new name.

3. (Optional) Select a different folder in the Save In list box to save the document in a different folder.

4. Click Save. Word saves the document under the new name.

USING DOCUMENT PROPERTIES

Every Word document has a set of properties that provide information about the document. Some properties contain summary information that you enter, while others contain information that is automatically generated by Word. To enter or view a document's properties:

1. Click File, Properties to open the Properties dialog box.

2. Click the Summary tab, as shown in Figure 4.2.

3. Enter or edit summary information as described in the following list.

4. Click OK. Document properties are saved along with the document.

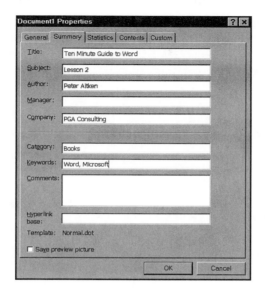

FIGURE 4.2   Entering document summary information.

These are the summary information properties you will use most often:

- Title   Enter the title of the document. This is not the same as the document's file name.

- Subject   Enter a phrase that describes the subject of the document.

- Author   Word automatically fills this field with the user name you entered when you installed the program. You can change it if necessary.

- Company   Your company name. This may be automatically entered for you based on your Windows installation.

- Category   Enter a word or phrase that describes the type of document.

- Keywords   Enter one or more words related to the document contents.

- Comments   Enter any additional information you want saved with the document.

Word automatically generates useful statistics about each document, such as the number of words it contains and the date and time the document was created. To view a document's statistics, click File, Properties then click the Statistics tab.

> **Quick Word Count** To get a quick count of the words and other elements in your document, click Tools, Word Count.

OPENING A DOCUMENT

You can open any document created with Word for Windows to continue working on it. You can also open documents that were created with other programs, such as WordPerfect.

To do so, click File, Open or click the Open button on the Standard toolbar. The Open dialog box appears, as shown in Figure 4.3.

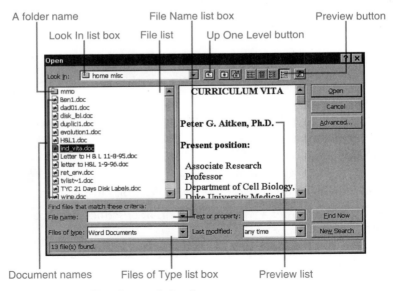

A folder name   File Name list box   Preview button

Look In list box   File list   Up One Level button

Document names   Files of Type list box   Preview list

FIGURE 4.3   The Open dialog box.

The file list shows all of the Word documents and folders in the current folder. Documents are identified by a small page icon next to their name, while folders display a file folder icon. The Look In list box shows the name of the current folder. You can take the following actions in the Open dialog box:

- To open a file, click its name in the file list or type its name in the File Name list box. Press Enter or click the Open button. Or, you can simply double-click the file name.

- To preview the contents of a file, click the file name, then click the Preview button. Click the Preview button again to turn preview off.

- To look for files other than Word documents, click the Files of Type drop-down arrow and select the desired document type.

- To move up one folder, click the Up One Level button.

- To move down one level to a different folder, double-click the folder name in the file list.

- To move to another folder, click the Look In drop-down arrow and select the desired folder.

Folder   Windows uses folders to organize files on a disk. Before Windows 95, folders were called subdirectories.

Word on the Web   To open a Web document for editing in Word, select **HTML document** from the Files of Type list.

To quickly open a document you recently worked on, you can use Word's Recently Used File List rather than the Open dialog box. To view this list, open the File menu—the list is displayed at the bottom of the menu just above the Exit command. To open a file on the list, press the number corresponding to the file or click the file name with the mouse. This list displays the document files that you have saved most recently. If you have just installed Word, there will be no files displayed here, of course. If you have saved files and the list still doesn't display, see the next paragraph.

You can control how many files appear on the Recently Used File List, and whether the list appears at all. Click Tools, Options to open the Options dialog box. Click the General tab if necessary. Click the Recently Used File List check box to turn it on or off to control the display of the list. To change the number of files displayed in the list, enter a number in the Entries text box, or click the up/down arrows to change the existing entry. Click OK when you're finished.

Quick Open   You can open a Word document (and start Word if it is not already running) by double-clicking the document name or icon in the Windows Explorer or My Computer window.

In this lesson, you learned how to name your document, save it to disk, and enter summary information. You also learned how to open a document you saved earlier. The next lesson shows you how to use Word's online Help system.

Using the Help System

In this lesson, you learn how to use Word's online Help system and the Office Assistant.

Different Kinds of Help

Word has several methods by which you can get help. They can be divided into three categories:

- The Office Assistant, which offers advice about what you are doing and answers questions you ask.

- The Help Topics window, which provides a Table of Contents, Index, and search facility for the online Help information.

- What's This Help, which lets you get information about any item on the screen simply by clicking it.

Asking the Office Assistant

You have probably already met the Office Assistant; it's the paper clip character that pops up to give you advice. The Office Assistant is a very powerful Help system that keeps track of what you are doing and can make some very intelligent guesses about what information you need.

No Assistant? If you cannot find the Office Assistant, it probably has not been installed. You must repeat the installation procedure, as described on the inside front cover, this time specifying the Office Assistant as one of the installation options.

No More Answer Wizard   The Office Assistant replaces the Answer Wizard feature from Word for Windows 95.

TURNING THE OFFICE ASSISTANT ON OR OFF

By default, the Office Assistant is turned on and sits on top of whatever you're working on, as shown in Figure 5.1. You can turn Office Assistant off by clicking the Close (X) button in the upper-right corner of its window.

FIGURE 5.1   The Office Assistant appears in its own dialog box, on top of the Word window.

To turn the Office Assistant on again, click the Help button on the Standard toolbar or click Help, Microsoft Word Help.

THE KINDS OF HELP OFFICE ASSISTANT PROVIDES

When you first turn on the Office Assistant, a bubble appears next to (or above) it. The bubble asks you what kind of help you want (see Figure 5.2). You can do any of the following:

- Type a question in the text box provided to ask for help on a specific topic. (More on this shortly in the section "Asking the Office Assistant a Question.")

- Select one of the Office Assistant's "guesses" about what you need help with. These guesses are displayed in the Assistant under the What Would You Like to Do heading. Guesses are not displayed at all times.

- Click the Tips button to get any tips that the Office Assistant can provide for the task you're performing.

- Click the Options button to customize the way the Office Assistant works.

- Click Close to close the bubble (but leave the Office Assistant on-screen).

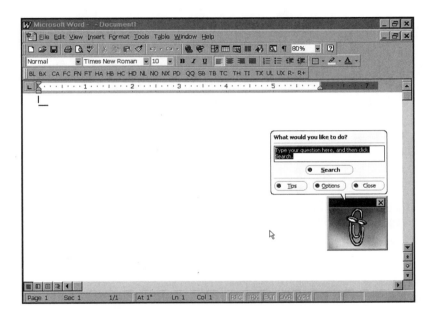

FIGURE 5.2   Office Assistant waiting for you to ask a question.

If you close the help bubble, you can reopen it at any time by clicking the Help button on the Standard toolbar; pressing F1; clicking Help, Microsoft Word Help; or clicking on the Office Assistant window.

ASKING THE OFFICE ASSISTANT A QUESTION

If you need help on a particular topic, simply type a question in the text box shown in Figure 5.2. Follow these steps:

1. If the Office Assistant's help bubble doesn't appear, click the Help button on the Standard toolbar.

2. Type a question in the text box. For example, you might type **How do I save?** to get help saving your work.

3. Click the Search button. The Office Assistant provides some topics that might match what you're looking for. For example, Figure 5.3 shows the Office Assistant's answer to the question "How do I save?"

FIGURE 5.3   The Office Assistant asks you to narrow down exactly what you are trying to accomplish, so it can provide the best help possible.

4. Click on the option that best describes what you're trying to do. For example, I'm going to choose Save a Document. A Help window appears with instructions for the specified task.

   If none of the options describe what you want, click the See More... arrow to view more options, or type a different question in the text box.

The Help window that appears containing the task instructions is part of the same Help system you can access using the Help, Contents and Index command, which is explained in the following section.

USING THE HELP TOPICS WINDOW

When you click Help, Contents and Index, the Help Topics window appears. The Help Topics window has three tabs, each corresponding to a different method for finding the information you need. These tabs are described in the following sections.

THE HELP TABLE OF CONTENTS

The Contents tab, shown in Figure 5.4, organizes the Help information by subject in a hierarchical fashion. At the top level is a series of *books*, each identified by a book icon next to the title. Each book can contain additional books as well as *topics*, which contain the Help information. A topic is identified by an icon of a page with a question mark on it.

FIGURE 5.4   The Contents tab in the Help Topics window.

On the Contents tab, you can perform the following actions:

- To open a book and display its contents, double-click the book's title. An open book has an open book icon next to it.

- To close a book and hide its contents, double-click the book's title.

- To open a topic, double-click its title.

- To print a topic, select the topic and click Print.

- To close the Help window, click the Cancel button or click the Close button on the title bar.

THE HELP INDEX

The Index tab in the Help Topics window provides another way to access Help information. As shown in Figure 5.5, the Index presents you with an alphabetical list of the available Help topics. You can scroll through the list to select a topic, or you can start typing a subject word in the text box and the list will automatically scroll to the first matching topic.

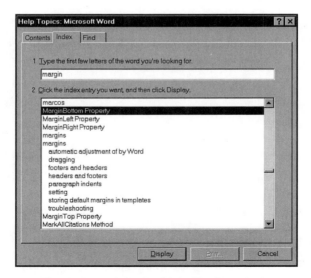

FIGURE 5.5   The Index tab in the Help Topics window.

After you find the topic you want, double-click it or select it and click the Display button. The topic information will be displayed in a topic window as described in the following section.

VIEWING A HELP TOPIC

Each Help topic contains different information, but each topic is organized in pretty much the same way. There are two basic types of Help topic screens. The one you'll see most often contains text (see Figure 5.6). Here are the actions you can take:

- Click an underlined term to view a definition of that term.

- Click a How button or a Show Me button to get more information on completing a specific task.

- Click the Back button to return to the previous Help topic you viewed (if any).

- Click the Help Topics button to return to the Contents tab of the Help Topics window.

- Click the Options button, then select Print Topic, to print the current topic.

- Press Esc or click the Close button in the upper-right corner of the title bar to close Help and return to your document.

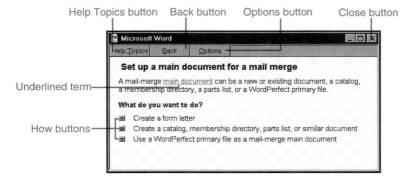

FIGURE 5.6   A text-based Help topic screen.

Another type of Help topic screen is graphics-based, with a picture of a document containing labels that identify the available Help topics (see Figure 5.7). To view a specific topic, click the corresponding label.

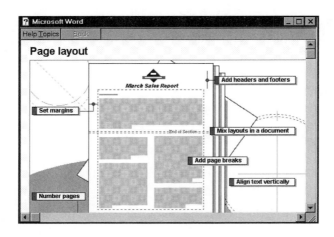

FIGURE 5.7   A graphics-based Help topic screen.

USING THE HELP TOPIC WINDOW'S FIND TAB

The Find tab of the Help Topics window lets you search through the online Help information for your topic of interest. You are not limited to Help topic titles, but can search every word in the entire Help system. You usually will use Find only when you have been unable to locate the needed information using the Contents and Index tabs.

The first time you use Find, it is necessary to build the list of words. You do this with the Find Setup Wizard, which automatically appears. On the first Wizard screen, click the default option, Minimize Database Size, then click Next followed by Finish. Building the list might take a few minutes, but you only need to do it once.

Figure 5.8 shows the Find tab. Here's how you use it:

1. Type the word or phrase you want to find in the Type the Word(s) You Want to Find text box.

2. Word automatically displays matching and related words in the Select Some Matching Words to Narrow Your Search list box. Initially, all of these words are selected (highlighted). To narrow the search, select the most relevant word by clicking it. To select two or more words in this list, hold down the Shift key while clicking.

3. The Click a Topic, Then Click Display list box lists the Help topics that match your search terms. Click the desired topic, then click Display.

FIGURE 5.8   The Find tab of the Help Topics window.

USING WHAT'S THIS HELP

Word's What's This Help feature lets you get Help about items that are visible on-screen. There are two ways to activate What's This Help:

- When a dialog box is open, click the question mark (?) button in the title bar.

- When a dialog box is not open, press Shift+F1 or click Help, What's This.

Either way, the mouse cursor will change to an arrow and a question mark. Click the screen item of interest to display a pop-up window with information about the selected item.

TIP **Word on the Web**   If you have an Internet connection, you can click Help, Microsoft on the Web, then select the desired subject, to be connected to Microsoft's related Web site.

In this lesson, you learned how to use Word's online Help system. The next lesson shows you how to find and replace text in your document.

Finding and Replacing Text

In this lesson, you learn how to find specific text in your document, and how to automatically replace it with new text.

Searching for Text

Word can search through your document to find occurrences of specific text. Word's default is to search the entire document, unless you select some text before you issue the command. If you select text first, the search will be limited to the selection.

If you want the search limited to part of the document, select the text first. Otherwise Word will search the entire document. Then, follow these steps:

1. Click Edit, Find or press Ctrl+F. The Find tab of the Find and Replace dialog box appears (see Figure 6.1).

2. In the Find What text box, enter the text you want to search for. The text you enter is the *search template*.

3. Click Find Next. Word looks through the document for text that matches the search template. If it finds matching text, it highlights it in the document and stops, with the Find and Replace dialog box still displayed.

4. Click Find Next to continue the search for another instance of the template. Or, press Esc to close the dialog box and return to the document. The found text remains selected.

When you have searched the entire document, or if the search template cannot be found, a message is displayed informing you of the search status.

TIP **Repeat Searches** When you open the Find and Replace dialog box, the previous search template (if any) will still be displayed in the Find What text box. This makes it easy to repeat the previous search.

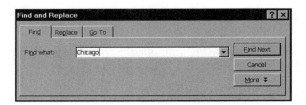

FIGURE 6.1   The Find tab of the Find and Replace dialog box.

 Search Template The search template is the model for the text you want to find.

USING SEARCH OPTIONS

The default Find operation locates the search template you specify without regard to the case of letters or whether it's a whole word or part of a word. For example, the template "the" will find "the," "THE," "mother," and so on. You can refine your search by using Word's search options. To do so, click the More button in the Find and Replace dialog box. The dialog box expands to offer additional options (see Figure 6.2).

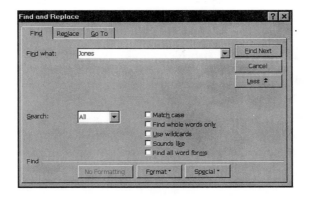

FIGURE 6.2   Setting options for the Find command.

You can choose from the following options:

- Match Case   Requires an exact match for upper- and lowercase letters. By selecting this check box, "The" will match only "The" and not "the" or "THE."

- Find Whole Words Only   This will match whole words only. By selecting this check box, "the" will match only "the"—not "mother," "these," and so on.

- Use Wildcards   Permits use of the * and ? wildcards in the search template. The * wildcard matches any sequence of 0 or more characters, while the ? wildcard matches any single character. The template "th?n" would match "thin," "then," but not "thrown" or "thn." The template "th*n" would match "thin," "thn," "thrown," and so on.

- Sounds Like   Finds words that sound similar to the template. By selecting this check box, for example, "their" will match "there."

- Find All Word Forms   Locates alternate forms of the search template. For example, "sit" will match not only "sit" but also "sat" and "sitting." This check box is not available if you select the Use Wildcards check box.

To control the extent of the search, click the Search drop-down arrow and select one of the following options:

- All   Searches the entire document.

- Down   Searches from the cursor to the end of the document.

- Up   Searches from the cursor to the start of the document.

Can't Find It?   If you can't find text that you're sure is in the document, check the spelling of the search template and make sure unwanted search options are not enabled.

Finding and Replacing Text

Word's Replace command lets you search for instances of text and replace them with new text. To replace text, click Edit, Replace or press Ctrl+H. The Replace tab of the Find and Replace dialog box appears (see Figure 6.3). Then:

Find or Replace   You can access the Find tab from the Replace tab, and *vice versa*, by clicking the corresponding tab.

1. In the Find What text box, enter the text you want to replace.

2. In the Replace With text box, enter the replacement text.

3. Click the More button (if necessary) and specify search options as explained in the previous section.

4. Click Find Next to locate and highlight the first instance of the target text. Then:

- Click Replace to replace the highlighted instance of the target text then locate the next instance of it.

- Click Find Next to leave the highlighted instance of the target text unchanged and to locate the next instance.

- Click Replace All to replace all instances of the target text in the entire document.

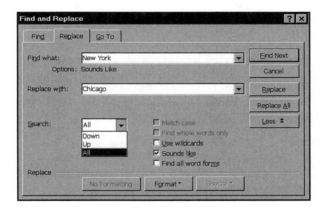

FIGURE 6.3   The Replace tab in the Find and Replace dialog box.

 Deleting Text   To delete the target text, follow the previous steps but leave the Replace With text box empty.

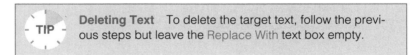 **Recovery!**   If you make a mistake replacing text, you can recover by clicking Edit, Undo Replace.

In this lesson, you learned how to search for and replace text in your document. In the next lesson, you will learn about Word's screen display options.

SCREEN DISPLAY OPTIONS

In this lesson, you learn how to control the Word screen display to suit your working style.

DOCUMENT DISPLAY OPTIONS

Word offers several ways to display your document. Each of these views is designed to make certain editing tasks easier. The available views are:

- Normal   Best for general editing tasks.

- Page Layout   Ideal for working with formatting and page layout.

- Online Layout   Optimized for viewing on-screen.

- Outline   Designed for working with outlines.

The view you use has no affect on the contents of your document or on the way it will look when printed. It affects only the way the document appears on screen.

NORMAL VIEW

Normal view is suitable for most editing tasks; it is the view you will probably use most often. This is Word's default view. All special formatting is visible on-screen, including different font sizes, italic, boldface, and other enhancements. The screen display appears essentially identical to how the document will appear when printed. Certain aspects of the page layout, however, do not appear to speed editing; for example, you do not see headers and footers or multiple columns. Figure 7.1 shows a document in Normal view.

To select Normal view, click View, Normal or click the Normal View button at the left end of the horizontal scroll bar.

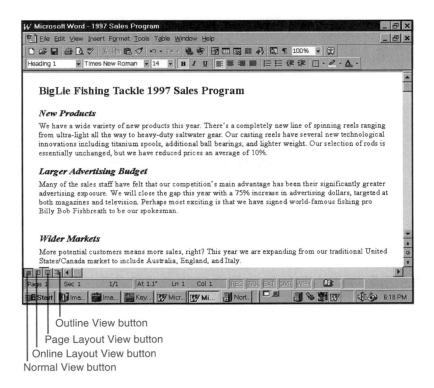

Outline View button
Page Layout View button
Online Layout View button
Normal View button

FIGURE 7.1   A document displayed in Normal view.

PAGE LAYOUT VIEW

Page Layout view displays your document exactly as it will print. Headers, footers, and all other details of the page layout appear on-screen. You can edit in Page Layout view; it's ideal for fine-tuning the details of page composition. Be aware, however, that the additional computer processing required makes display changes relatively slow in Page Layout view, particularly when you have a complex page layout. Figure 7.2 shows a sample document in Page Layout view.

TIP   **Sneak Preview**   Use Page Layout view to see what your printed document will look like before you actually print. The Print Preview feature, covered in Lesson 21, is preferred for previewing entire pages.

Header

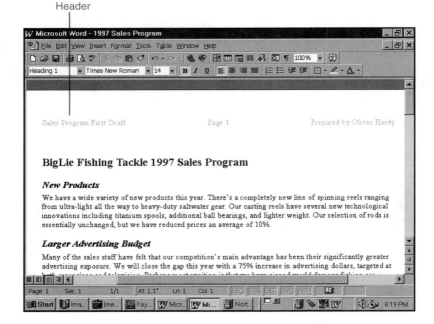

FIGURE 7.2   A document viewed in Page Layout view showing header display.

Click View, Page Layout (or click the Page Layout View button) to switch to Page Layout view.

ONLINE LAYOUT VIEW

Online Layout view is optimal for reading and editing a document on-screen. Legibility is increased by using larger fonts; displaying shorter lines of text; hiding headers, footers, and similar elements; and basing the layout on the screen rather than on the printed page. Also, the document map is displayed on the left side of the screen (the document map is covered later in this lesson). The screen display will not match the final printed appearance. Online Layout view is ideal for editing the document text, but is not suited for working with page layout or graphics.

TIP   **Content Editing** Use Online Layout view when editing the document contents as opposed to its appearance.

Click View, Online Layout (or click the Online Layout View button) to switch to Online Layout view.

When you're in Online Layout view, the horizontal scroll bar and its View buttons are hidden. You must use the View menu commands to switch to a different view. Figure 7.3 shows a document in Online Layout view.

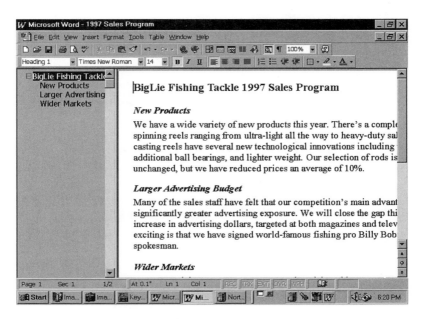

FIGURE 7.3   A document displayed in Online Layout view.

OUTLINE VIEW

Use Outline view to create outlines and to examine the structure of a document. Figure 7.4 shows a document in Outline view. In this view, you can choose to view only your document headings, thus hiding all subordinate text. You can quickly promote, demote, or move document headings along with subordinate text to a new location. For this view to be useful, you need to assign heading styles to the document headings, a technique you'll learn about in Lesson 13.

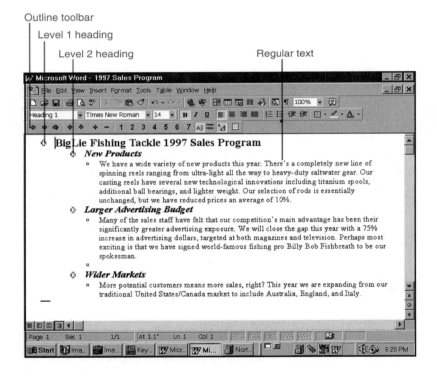

FIGURE 7.4   A document displayed in Outline view.

 Click View, Outline to switch to Outline view, or click the Outline View button at the left end of the horizontal scroll bar.

DRAFT FONT VIEW

Draft Font view is a display option you can apply in both Normal and Outline views. As you can see in Figure 7.5, Draft Font view uses a single generic font for all text; it indicates special formatting by underlining or boldface. Graphics display as empty boxes. Draft Font view provides the fastest editing and screen display, and is particularly useful when editing the content of documents that contain a lot of fancy formatting and graphics. This view is ideal when you're concentrating on the contents of your document rather than its appearance.

To turn Draft Font view on or off:

1. Click Tools, Options to open the Options dialog box.

2. If necessary, click the View tab to display the View options.

3. Select the Draft Font check box to turn it on or off.

4. Select OK.

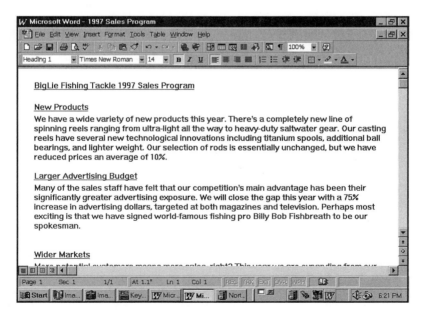

FIGURE 7.5 A document displayed in Draft Font view.

Full Screen View

Full Screen view provides the maximum amount of screen real estate to display your document contents. In Full Screen view, the title bar, menu, toolbars, Status bar, and all other Word elements are hidden, and your document occupies the entire screen. You use Full Screen view in combination with other views. Thus, you can use Full Screen view in Normal view, Page Layout view, and so on. You can enter and edit text in this view and select from the menus using the usual keyboard commands. To turn on Full Screen view, click View, Full Screen. To turn off Full Screen view, select View, Full Screen again (using the keyboard), or click the Close Full Screen box that appears in the lower-right corner of the screen.

Zooming the Screen

The Zoom command lets you control the size of your document on-screen. You can enlarge it to facilitate reading small fonts or decrease it to view an entire page at one time. Click View, Zoom to open the Zoom dialog box (see Figure 7.6).

The following options are available in the Zoom dialog box. As you make selections, the Preview area shows you what the selected zoom setting will look like.

- Select 200%, 100%, or 75% to zoom to the indicated magnification. 200% is twice normal size, 75% is three-quarters normal size, and so on.

- Enter a custom magnification in the range 10-200 percent in the Percent text box.

- Select Page Width to scale the display to fit the entire page width on-screen.

- Select Whole Page to scale the display to fit the entire page, vertically and horizontally, on-screen.

- Select Many Pages to display two or more pages at the same time. Click the Monitor button under the Many Pages option, and then drag to specify how many pages to display.

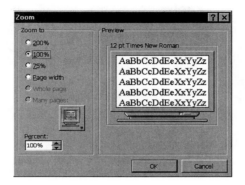

FIGURE 7.6   The Zoom dialog box.

The Whole Page and Many Pages options are available only if you are viewing the document in Page Layout view.

Quick Zoom   You can quickly change the zoom setting by clicking the Zoom drop-down arrow on the Standard toolbar and selecting the desired zoom setting from the list (refer to Figure 7.6).

USING THE DOCUMENT MAP

The Document Map is a separate pane that displays your document's headings. You do not edit in the Document Map, but rather use it to quickly move around your document. The document map is displayed automatically when you switch to Online Layout view. You can also display it in other views by clicking View, Document Map. Figure 7.7 shows a document with the map displayed.

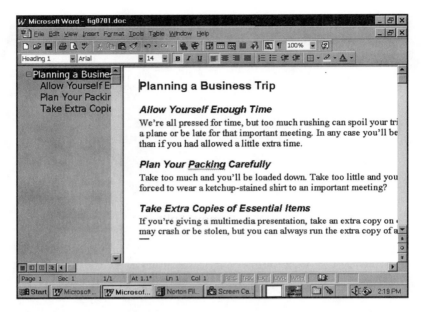

Figure 7.7   The Document Map is displayed to the left of the work area.

To use the document map, simply click the desired map heading and the main document window will scroll to that location in the document. You can control the width of the map display by pointing at the border between the map and the document and dragging it to the desired location. Dragging the border to the left edge of the screen has the same effect as turning the Document Map off.

Splitting the Screen

Word lets you split the work area into two panels, one above the other, so you can view different parts of one document at the same time. Each panel scrolls independently and has its own scroll bars. Figure 7.8 shows a document displayed on a split screen. Editing changes that you make in either panel affect the document. To split the screen:

1. Click Window, Split or press Ctrl+Alt+S. Word displays a horizontal splitter bar across the middle of the work area.

2. To accept two equal size panes, click with the left mouse button or press Enter. To create different size panes, move the mouse until the splitter bar is in the desired location then click or press Enter.

When working with a split screen, you move the editing cursor from one pane to the other by clicking with the mouse. To change the pane sizes, point at the splitter bar and drag it to the new location. To remove the splitter bar and return to regular view, drag the splitter bar to either the top or the bottom of the work area, or click Windows, Remove Split.

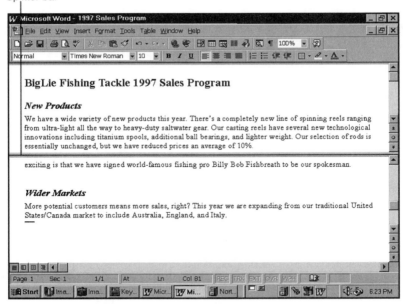

Splitter bar

FIGURE 7.8 Viewing a document in split screen view.

Quick Split   You can quickly split the screen by pointing at the splitter bar, just above the up arrow on the vertical toolbar (refer to Figure 7.8) and dragging it down to the desired location.

In this lesson, you learned how to control Word's screen display. In the next lesson, you'll learn how to print and fax your documents.

PRINTING, MAILING, AND FAXING YOUR DOCUMENT

In this lesson, you learn how to print your document, how to send it via e-mail, and how to send a document via fax.

PRINTING USING THE DEFAULT SETTINGS

It's very simple to print using the default settings. This means to print a single copy of the entire document on the default Windows printer. To do so:

1. Click File, Print, or press Ctrl+P. The Print dialog box appears (see Figure 8.1).

2. Click OK. The document prints.

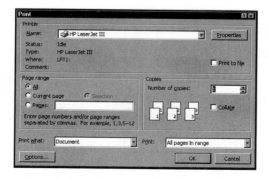

FIGURE 8.1   The Print dialog box.

Quick Printing To print without going to the Print dialog box, click the Print button on the Standard toolbar.

Printer Not Working? Refer to your Microsoft Windows and printer documentation for help. If you're using a network printer, see your network administrator.

PRINTING MULTIPLE COPIES

You can print more than one copy of a document, and you can specify that the copies be collated. To print multiple copies:

1. Click File, Print, or press Ctrl+P. The Print dialog box appears (refer to Figure 8.1).

2. In the Number of Copies box, enter the desired number of copies. Or, click the incrementer arrows to set the desired value.

3. Select the Collate check box to turn it on or off.

4. Click OK.

More than One Printer? If you have two or more printers installed, you can select the one to use by clicking the Name drop-down arrow at the top of the Print dialog box and selecting the desired printer from the list.

PRINTING PART OF A DOCUMENT

Most often you will want to print all of a document. You can, however, print just part of a document, ranging from a single sentence to multiple pages. Follow these steps:

1. To print a section of text, select the text. To print a single page, move the cursor to that page.

2. Click File, Print, or press Ctrl+P. The Print dialog box appears (refer to Figure 8.1).

3. In the Page Range area, specify what should be printed:

    • Choose Selection to print the selected text.

    • Choose Current Page to print the page containing the cursor.

    • Choose Pages to print specified pages, then enter the page numbers in the text box. For example, entering 1-3 will print pages 1 through 3, and entering 2,4 will print pages 2 and 4.

4. Click OK.

Printing Properties To print a document's properties rather than its text, click the Print What drop-down arrow in the Print dialog box and select Document Properties from the list.

CHANGING YOUR PRINT OPTIONS

Word offers a number of printing options that you may need to use at times. You can print only the odd-numbered pages or only the even-numbered pages. This option is useful to create two-sided output on a standard one-sided printer: print the odd-numbered pages, then flip the printed pages over and place them back in the printer's paper tray and print the even-numbered pages. You select which pages to print by clicking the Print drop-down arrow in the Print dialog box and selecting Odd Pages or Even Pages from the list. Select All Pages in Range to return to printing all pages.

You set other print options in the Print dialog box (see Figure 8.2). To display this dialog box, open the Print dialog box as previously described and click the Options button.

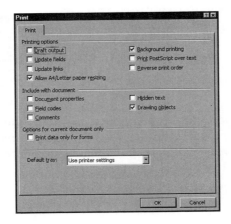

FIGURE 8.2   The Print dialog box.

The options you will use most often are described here:

- Draft Output   Produces draft output that prints faster but may lack some graphics and formatting (depending on your specific printer).

- Reverse Print Order   Prints pages in last-to-first order. This setting produces collated output on printers that have face-up output.

- Background Printing   Permits you to continue working on the document while printing is in progress. This setting uses additional memory and usually results in slower printing.

- Update Fields   Updates the contents of all document fields before printing.

- Document Properties   Prints the document's properties in addition to its contents.

- Comments   Includes document comments in the printout.

After setting the desired printing options, click OK to return to the Print dialog box.

 Save Paper! Use Page Layout view to check the appearance of your document before printing it.

FAXING A DOCUMENT

If your system is set up for fax, you can fax a document directly to one or more recipients without having to print a paper copy and feed it into a standard fax machine. This saves both time and paper. To fax the current document:

1. Click File, Send To, Fax Recipient.

2. Word starts the Fax Wizard, which will take you through the steps of preparing the fax, choosing a cover page, and selecting recipients. After entering the requested information at each step, click Next. After the final step, click Finish.

3. If you requested a cover sheet, Word displays it. You can make any additions or changes to the cover sheet at this time.

4. Click the Send Fax Now button to send the Fax.

 No Fax Option? If the Fax Recipient option is not available on your Send To submenu, it means that your system has not been set up for faxing.

 Another Way to Fax You can also fax a document by selecting Microsoft Fax (or the name of whatever fax program you use) as the destination printer in the Print dialog box, then printing in the usual fashion.

MAILING A DOCUMENT

If you have Microsoft Messaging or another e-mail program installed on your system, you can send a document directly to a mail recipient. Here are the steps to take:

1. Click File, Send To, Mail Recipient.

2. Depending on the specifics of your system, Word may ask you to select a profile setting. Generally, the default setting is the one you should select.

3. Next, you will see your usual New Message window. The appearance of this window will vary depending on the mail system you are using, but it will be the same mail form that you use for other e-mail messages. Figure 8.3 shows the New Message window used by the Windows Messaging system.

4. The document will already be inserted in the message as an icon. You can add text to the message if desired. You must also fill in the To... text box of the message with the recipient's address.

5. When the message is complete, click the Send button.

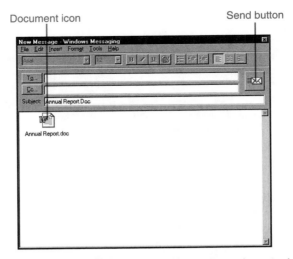

FIGURE 8.3   A new message with the document inserted as an icon.

When the recipient receives your message, he will be able to double-click the document icon to open the document in Word for printing, editing, and so on.

In this lesson, you learned how to print your document, and how to send it as a fax or as an e-mail message. The next lesson shows you how to use fonts, borders, and shading in your document.

FONTS, BORDERS, AND SHADING

*In this lesson, you learn how to use different fonts
in your document, and how to apply borders and shading.*

FONT TERMINOLOGY

Word offers you a huge assortment of fonts to use in your documents. Each font has a specific *typeface*, which determines the appearance of the characters. Typefaces are identified by names such as Arial, Courier, and Times New Roman. Each font also has a size, which is specified in *points*. One point is equal to 1/72 of an inch, so a 36 point font would have its largest characters 1/2 inch tall. Most documents use font sizes in the 8 to 14 point range, but the larger and smaller sizes are available for headings and other special needs.

SELECTING A FONT

You can change the font of text that already has been typed by first selecting the text. To specify the font for text you are about to type, simply move the cursor to the desired location. Then:

1. Click Format, Font to open the Font dialog box, shown in Figure 9.1.

2. The Font list displays the name of the current font. Scroll through the list and select the new font name.

3. The Size list displays the current font size. Select the new size from the list or type a number in the text box. The Preview box shows the appearance of the selected font.

4. Select OK.

Quick Select Remember, you can select an entire document by pressing Ctrl+A.

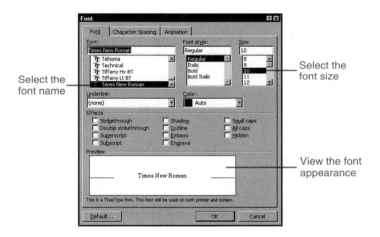

Select the font name

Select the font size

View the font appearance

FIGURE 9.1 The Font dialog box.

You can quickly select a font name and size using the Formatting toolbar. The Font list box and the Font Size list box display the name and size of the current font. You can change the font by clicking the drop-down arrows of either list and making a selection. Note that in the Font list, the fonts you have used recently are placed at the top of the list.

Keyboard Happy? You can use the keyboard to access the Font and Font Size lists on the toolbar by pressing Ctrl+Shift+F or Ctrl+Shift+P followed by the down arrow.

USING BOLDFACE, ITALICS, AND UNDERLINING

You can display any of Word's fonts in boldface, italics, or underlined. You can also use two or three of these effects in combination. As with other formatting, you can apply these effects to existing text by first selecting the text, or to text you are about to type.

 The quickest way to assign boldface, italics, or underlining is with the buttons on the Formatting toolbar. Click a button to turn the corresponding attribute on; click it again to turn it off. When the cursor is at a location where one of these attributes is turned on, the corresponding toolbar button will appear depressed.

You can also assign font attributes using the Font dialog box. If you want to use underlining other than the default single underline, you must use this method. Here's how:

1. Click Format, Font to open the Font dialog box (refer to Figure 9.1).

2. Under Font Style, select Bold, Italic, or Bold Italic. Select Regular to return to normal text.

3. Click the Underline drop-down arrow and select the desired underline style from the list, or select (none) to remove underlining.

4. Select OK.

TIP **A New Default** To change the default font used in documents based on the Normal template, open the Font dialog box, select the desired font and attributes, and click the Default button.

APPLYING SPECIAL FONT EFFECTS

Word has a number of special font effects that you can use. These include superscript and subscript, strikethrough, and several graphics effects such as shadow and outline. You can also specify that text be hidden, which means it will not display on-screen or be printed. To assign special font effects to selected text or text you are about to type:

1. Click Format, Font to open the Font dialog box (refer to Figure 9.1).

2. In the Effects area, select the effects you want. To remove an effect, deselect the check box. The Preview box shows you what the selected effects will look like.

3. Select OK.

Where's that Hidden Text? To locate hidden text, click Tools, Options, click the View tab, then select the Hidden Text option. Hidden text will display with a dotted underline. You can also display hidden text by clicking the Show/Hide ¶ button.

DISPLAYING BORDERS

Word's Borders command lets you improve the appearance of your documents by displaying borders around selected text. Figure 9.2 shows examples of the use of borders (and illustrates shading, covered in the section "Applying Shading" later in this lesson).

 You can apply a border to selected text or to individual paragraphs. To put a border around text, select the text. For a paragraph, place the cursor anywhere in the paragraph. The quickest way to apply a border is to use the Border button on the Formatting toolbar. Click the arrow next to the button to view a palette of available border settings, then click the desired border diagram. Click the No Borders diagram to remove borders.

Shading   Border

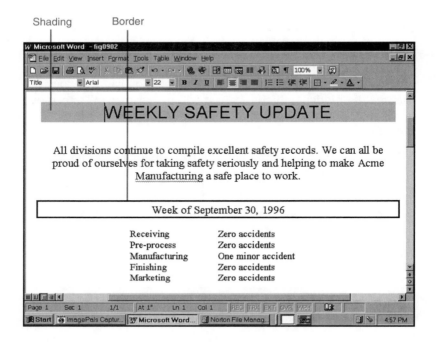

FIGURE **9.2**   A document with a border and shading.

If you need more control over the appearance of your borders, you must use the Borders and Shading dialog box (see Figure 9.3). To open this dialog box, click Format, Borders and Shading then click the Borders tab if necessary.

The steps for creating a border are as follows:

1. Select the general appearance of the borders you want by clicking the corresponding icon in the Setting area (the Custom setting is explained below).

2. Select the desired line style from the Style list; the desired color from the Color list; and the desired width from the Width list.

3. In the Preview area, click the buttons or click directly on the page diagram to add or remove borders from the four sides of the text.

4. If you selected text before opening the dialog box, use the Apply To list to specify whether the border is to be displayed around the selected text or the current paragraph.

5. Click OK.

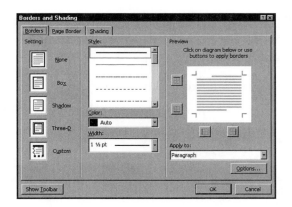

FIGURE 9.3   The Borders tab of the Borders and Shading dialog box.

The normal border settings apply the same line style (solid, dotted, and so on) to all four sides of the border box. To create a custom border that combines different styles:

1. Click the Custom icon.

2. Select the line style, color, and width for one side of the border.

3. In the Preview area, click the button or click directly on the page diagram to specify the side of the border you want the style used for.

4. Repeat steps 2 and 3 to specify the style for the other three sides of the border.

5. Select OK.

You can also place borders around entire pages in your document. To do so, click the Page Border tab of the Borders and Shading dialog box. This tab looks and operates just as the Borders tab does in terms of specifying the border's appearance. The only difference is specifying where the border will be applied, which is done with the Apply To list. You have four choices:

- Whole Document

- This Section

- This Section - First Page Only

- This Section - All Except First Page

You'll learn how to divide a document into sections in Lesson 13.

APPLYING SHADING

You can use shading to display text over a background color, such as black text on a light gray background. Figure 9.2 showed an example of shading. You can apply shading to selected text or to individual paragraphs. Shading is comprised of either a fill color, a pattern color, or a combination of both. Here's how to apply shading:

1. Select the text to be shaded, or position the cursor anywhere in the paragraph to shade an entire paragraph.

2. Click Format, Borders and Shading to open the Borders and Shading dialog box. Click the Shading tab (see Figure 9.4).

3. To use a fill color, select it from the palette in the Fill area of the dialog box. To use only a pattern color, select None.

4. To use a pattern color, select its style and color from the lists in the Patterns section of the dialog box. To use only a fill color, select the Clear style. You can view the appearance of the selected settings in the Preview area of the dialog box.

5. If you selected text before opening the dialog box, use the Apply To list to specify whether the fill should apply to the select text or the current paragraph.

6. Select OK.

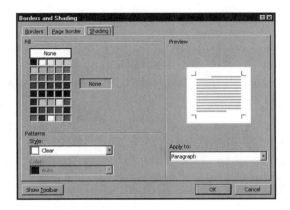

FIGURE 9.4   The Shading tab of the Borders and Shading dialog box.

Printing Color?   Of course, color shading will print in color only if you have a color printer. You need to perform test printouts of pages with shading because screen display of shading is often quite different from the final printed results.

This lesson showed you how to use fonts, borders, and shading in your documents. The next lesson teaches you how to control indentation and justification of text, and how to control line breaks.

INDENTS AND
JUSTIFICATION

In this lesson, you learn how to set the indentation and justification of text in your document, and how to control line breaks.

INDENTATION

The distance between your text and the left and right edges of the page is controlled by two things: the left and right page margins and the text indentation. Margins, which are covered in Lesson 13, are usually changed only for entire documents or large sections of a document. For smaller sections of text, such as individual lines and paragraphs, you will use indentation.

 Indentation The distance between a paragraph's text and the margins for the entire document. For example, if the left margin is set at 1" and a paragraph has a 1" indentation, that paragraph starts 2" from the edge of the paper.

The easiest way to set indents is by using the Ruler and your mouse. To display the Ruler (or hide it), click View, Ruler. The numbers on the Ruler indicate the space from the left margin in inches. Figure 10.1 shows the Ruler and identifies the various elements you use to set indents. It also illustrates the various indent options.

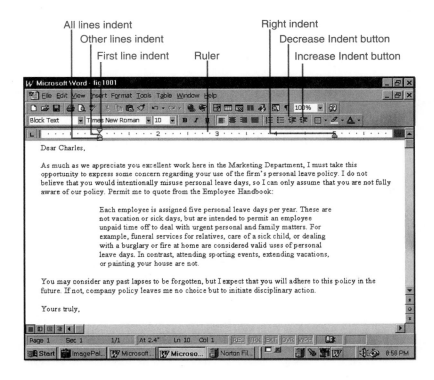

FIGURE 10.1   Using the Ruler to set text indentation. The second paragraph is indented one inch from both the right and left margins.

Indentation applies to individual paragraphs. To set indentation for one paragraph, position the cursor anywhere in the paragraph. For more than one paragraph, select the paragraphs. (Otherwise, the new indents will apply only to new paragraphs that you type from the insertion point forward.) Then drag the indent markers on the Ruler to the desired positions. As you drag, a dotted vertical line displays down the document to show the new indent location.

- To change the indent of the first line of a paragraph, drag the First Line Indent marker to the desired position.

- To change the indent of all lines of a paragraph, except the first one, drag the Other Lines Indent marker to the desired position (this is called a hanging indent).

- To change the indent of all lines of a paragraph, drag the All Lines Indent marker to the desired position.

- To change the indent of the right edge of the paragraph, drag the Right Indent marker to the desired position.

 You can also quickly increase or decrease (by 1/2 inch) the left indent of the current paragraph by clicking the Increase Indent or Decrease Indent buttons on the Formatting toolbar. The quickest way to indent the first line of a paragraph is to position the cursor at the start of the line and press Tab.

> **Rapid Ruler** Quickly display the Ruler by positioning the mouse pointer at the top edge of the work area for a moment. After you're done using the Ruler and move the mouse pointer away, the Ruler will automatically be hidden again.
>
> — TIP

 Hanging Indent A paragraph in which the first line is indented less than all the other lines.

SETTING INDENTS WITH THE PARAGRAPHS DIALOG BOX

Word also gives you the option of setting indents using the Paragraphs dialog box:

1. Click Format, Paragraph to open the Paragraph dialog box, then click the Indents and Spacing tab if necessary to display the indents and spacing options (see Figure 10.2).

2. Under Indentation, click the incrementer arrows of the Left or Right text boxes to increase or decrease the indentation settings. For a first line or a hanging indent, select the indent type in the Special drop-down list, then enter the indent amount in the By text box. The sample page in the dialog box illustrates how the current settings will appear.

3. Click OK. The new settings are applied to any selected paragraphs or to new text.

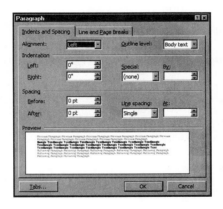

FIGURE 10.2   Setting indents in the Paragraph dialog box.

GETTING TEXT JUSTIFICATION

Justification, sometimes called alignment, refers to the manner in which the left and right ends of lines of text are aligned. Word offers four justification options:

- Left justification aligns the left ends of lines.

- Right justification aligns the right ends of lines.

- Full justification aligns both the left and right ends of lines.

- Center justification centers lines between the left and right margins.

Full Justification Both the left and right edges or paragraphs are aligned. This is accomplished by inserting extra space between words and letters in the text as needed.

Figure 10.3 illustrates the justification options. To change the justification for one or more paragraphs, first select the paragraphs to change; then, click one of the justification buttons on the Formatting toolbar.

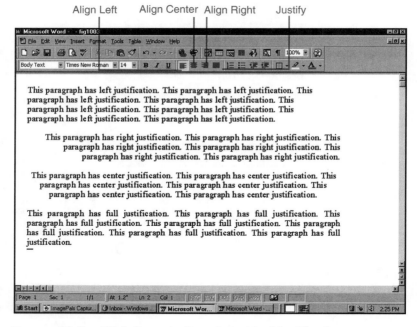

FIGURE 10.3   Click these buttons to set text justification.

If you prefer to use a dialog box to change justification, select the paragraphs and then:

1. Click Format, Paragraph to open the Paragraph dialog box, and click the Indents and Spacing tab if necessary.

2. Click the Alignment drop-down arrow and select the desired alignment from the list.

3. Select OK.

TIP

How Is it Justified? The toolbar button corresponding to the current paragraph's justification setting appears depressed.

CONTROLLING LINE BREAKS

The word wrap feature automatically breaks each line in a paragraph when it reaches the right margin. Word offers a couple of methods for controlling the way lines break. You can prevent a line break from occurring between two specific words, thus ensuring that the words always remain together on the same line. These methods can be particularly useful when you modify indents and justification because this often changes where individual lines break.

Word's default is to break lines as needed at spaces or hyphens. To prevent a line break, you must insert a non-breaking space or a non-breaking hyphen instead. To insert a non-breaking hyphen, press Ctrl+Shift+ - (hyphen). To insert a non-breaking space, press Ctrl+Shift+spacebar.

You can also use an *optional hyphen* to specify where a word can be broken, if necessary. This is useful with long words that may fall at the end of the line; if word wrap moves the long word to the next line, there will be an unsightly gap at the end of the previous line. An optional hyphen remains hidden unless the word extends past the right margin. Then, the hyphen appears and only the part of the word after the hyphen wraps to the new line. To insert an optional hyphen, press Ctrl+ - (hyphen).

Finally, you can insert a line break without starting a new paragraph by pressing Shift+Enter.

In this lesson, you learned how to set the indentation and justification of text in your document, and how to control line breaks. The next lesson shows you how to work with tabs and line spacing.

TABS AND LINE SPACING

In this lesson, you learn how to use and set tab stops, and how to change line spacing.

WHAT ARE TABS?

Tabs provide a way for you to control the indentation and vertical alignment of text in your document. When you press the Tab key, Word inserts a tab in the document, which moves the cursor (and any text to the right of it) to the next tab stop. By default, Word has tab stops at 0.5-inch intervals across the width of the page. You can modify the location of tab stops and control the way text aligns at a tab stop.

TYPES OF TAB STOPS

There are four types of tab stops; each aligns text differently:

- **Left-aligned**   The left edge of text aligns at the tab stop. Word's default tab stops are left-aligned.

- **Right-aligned**   The right edge of text aligns at the tab stop.

- **Center-aligned**   The text is centered at the tab stop.

- **Decimal-aligned**   The decimal point (period) is aligned at the tab stop. You use this type of tab for aligning columns of numbers.

Figure 11.1 illustrates the effects of the four tab alignment options and shows the four markers that appear on the Ruler to indicate the position of tab stops.

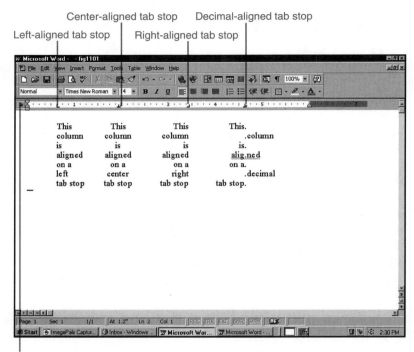

Center-aligned tab stop   Decimal-aligned tab stop
Left-aligned tab stop   Right-aligned tab stop

Click here until it shows the marker for the type of tab you want.

FIGURE 11.1   The four tab stop alignment options.

CHANGING THE DEFAULT TAB STOPS

Default tab stops affect all paragraphs for which you have not set custom tab stops (covered in the next section). You cannot delete the default tab stops, but you can change the spacing between them. The default tab stop spacing affects the entire document. Here are the steps to follow:

1. Click Format, Tabs to display the Tabs dialog box, as shown in Figure 11.2.

2. In the Default Tab Stops box, click the incrementer arrows to increase or decrease the spacing between default tab stops.

3. Click OK.

FIGURE 11.2   The Tabs dialog box.

Good-bye Tabs   To effectively "delete" all the default tab stops, set the spacing between them to a value larger than the page width.

CREATING CUSTOM TAB STOPS

If the default tab stops are not suited to your needs, you can add custom tab stops. The number, spacing, and type of custom tab stops is totally up to you.

1. Select the paragraphs that will have custom tabs. If no text is selected, the new tabs will affect the paragraph containing the cursor and the new text you type.

2. Click the tab symbol at the left end of the Ruler until it displays the marker for the type of tab you want to insert (refer to Figure 11.1).

3. Point at the approximate tab stop location on the Ruler, and press and hold the left mouse button. A dashed vertical line will extend down through the document showing the tab stop position relative to your text.

4. Move the mouse left or right until the tab stop is at the desired location.

5. Release the mouse button.

No Ruler?   If your Ruler is not displayed, click View, Ruler or position the mouse pointer near the top edge of the work area for a few seconds.

When you add a custom tab stop, all of the default tab stops to the left are temporarily inactivated. This ensures that the custom tab stop will take precedence. If custom tab stops have been defined for the current paragraph, then the custom tabs are displayed on the Ruler; otherwise, the default tab stops are displayed.

MOVING AND DELETING CUSTOM TAB STOPS

Follow these steps to move a custom tab stop to a new position:

1. Point at the tab stop marker on the Ruler.

2. Press and hold the left mouse button.

3. Drag the tab stop to the new position.

4. Release the mouse button.

To delete a custom tab stop, follow the same steps, but, in step 3, drag the tab stop marker off the Ruler, then release the mouse button.

CHANGING LINE SPACING

Line spacing controls the amount of vertical space between lines of text. Different spacing is appropriate for different kinds of documents. If you want to print your document on as few pages as possible, use single line spacing to position lines close together. In contrast, a document that will later be edited by hand should be printed with wide line spacing to provide space for the editor to write comments.

Word offers a variety of line spacing options. If you change line spacing, it affects the selected text; if there is no text selected, it affects the current paragraph and text you type at the insertion point. To change line spacing:

1. Click Format, Paragraph to open the Paragraph dialog box. If necessary, click the Indents and Spacing tab (see Figure 11.3).

2. Click the Line Spacing drop-down arrow and select the desired spacing from the list. The **Single**, **1.5 Lines**, and **Double** settings are self-explanatory. The other settings are:

   - **Exactly** Space between lines will be exactly the value, in points, that you enter in the At text box.

   - **At Least** Space between lines will be at least the value you enter in the At text box; Word will increase the spacing as needed if the line contains large characters.

   - **Multiple** Changes spacing by the factor you enter in the At text box. For example, enter **1.5** to increase spacing by one and a half times, and enter **2** to double the line spacing.

 Underline Missing? If you set line spacing using the Exactly option at the same value as your font size, then underline will display only for the last line of each paragraph.

3. To add spacing before the first line, or after the last line, of the paragraph, enter the desired space (in points) or click the arrows in the Before and After text boxes.

4. Click OK.

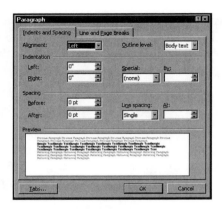

FIGURE 11.3   The Paragraph dialog box with the Indents and Spacing options displayed.

In this lesson, you learned how to use and set tab stops, and how to change line spacing. The next lesson shows you how to use styles.

MAKING THE MOST OF STYLES

In this lesson, you learn how to use styles in your documents.

UNDERSTANDING STYLES

Word's styles provide a great deal of power and flexibility when it comes to formatting your document. A *style* is a collection of formatting specifications that has been assigned a name and saved. For example, a given style could specify 14-point Arial font, 1-inch indent, double line spacing, and full justification. After you define a style, you can quickly apply it to any text in your document. Applying a style is a lot faster than manually applying individual formatting elements, and has the added advantage of assuring consistency. If you later modify a style definition, all of the text in the document to which that style has been assigned will automatically change to reflect the new style formatting. Word has several predefined styles, and you can create your own.

What Is a Style? A style is a named grouping of paragraph or character formatting that can be reused.

Word has two types of styles:

- *Paragraph* styles apply to entire paragraphs, and can include all aspects of formatting that affect a paragraph's appearance: font, line spacing, indents, tab stops, borders, and so on. Every paragraph has a style; the default paragraph style is called Normal.

- *Character* styles apply to any section of text, and can include any formatting that applies to individual characters—font name and size, underlining, boldface, and so on. In other words, any of the formats that you can assign by clicking Format, Font. There is no default character style.

When you apply a character style, the formatting is applied in addition to whatever formatting the text already possesses. For example, if you apply a character style defined as boldface to a sentence that is already formatted as italic, the word will display in boldface italic. The uses of styles are covered in this lesson and the next one.

ASSIGNING A STYLE TO TEXT

To assign a paragraph style to multiple paragraphs, select the paragraphs. To assign a paragraph style to a single paragraph, place the cursor anywhere inside the paragraph. To assign a character style, select the text you want the style to affect. Then:

1. Click the Style drop-down arrow on the Formatting toolbar to see a list of available styles, with each style name displayed in the style's font. Symbols in the list also indicate whether a style is a paragraph or character style as well as its font size and justification (see Figure 12.1).

2. Select the desired style by clicking its name. The style is applied to the specified text.

 TIP   **Paragraph or Character Style?**   In the Style list, paragraph styles are listed with the paragraph symbol next to them, and character styles are listed with an underlined letter "a" next to them.

To remove a character style from text, select the text and apply the character style Default Paragraph Font. This is not really a style, but rather specifies that the formatting defined in the current paragraph style should be used for the text.

Style list   Style name

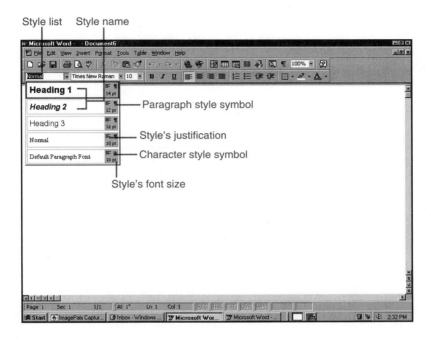

FIGURE 12.1   You select a style from the Style list on the Formatting toolbar.

VIEWING STYLE NAMES

The Style list displays the name of the style assigned to the text where the insertion point is located. If there is text selected or if the insertion point is in text that has a character style applied, then the Style list displays the character style name. Otherwise it displays the paragraph style of the current paragraph.

Word can also display the name of the paragraph and character styles assigned to specific text in your document. To do so:

1. Press Shift+F1 or click Help, What's This to activate What's This Help. The mouse cursor will display a question mark.

2. Click the text of interest. Word displays information about the text's style assignment in a balloon, as shown in Figure 12.2.

3. Repeat step 2 as needed for other text.

4. Press Esc when you are done.

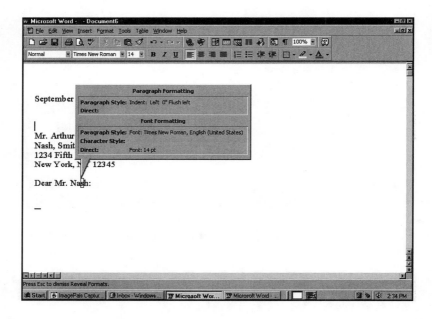

FIGURE 12.2 Displaying text style information with What's This Help.

CREATING A NEW STYLE

You are not limited to using Word's predefined styles. In fact, creating your own styles is an essential part of getting the most out of Word's style capabilities. One way to create a new style is "by example," as follows:

1. Find a paragraph that you want the new style applied to.

2. Format the paragraph as desired. In other words, apply the formatting you want included in the new style definition.

3. With the insertion point anywhere in the paragraph, click the Style drop-down arrow or press Ctrl+Shift+S (both activate the Style list).

4. Type the new style name and press Enter.

In step 4, don't enter the name of an existing style. If you do, that style's formatting will be applied to the paragraph and the formatting changes you made will be lost. If this happens, you can recover the formatting by clicking Edit, Undo, then repeat steps 3 and 4 with a new style name.

You can also create a new style by making formatting entries in dialog boxes. You must use this method to create a character style; it is optional for paragraph styles. You can create a new style from scratch, or you can base it on an existing style. If you choose the latter method, the new style will have all of the formatting of the base style plus any additions and changes you make while defining the style. Here are the required steps:

1. Click Format, Style to open the Style dialog box.

2. Click the New button. The New Style dialog box appears (see Figure 12.3).

3. Click the Style Type drop-down arrow and select Character or Paragraph from the list, depending on the type of style you're creating.

4. Click the Name text box and type the name for the new style.

5. If you want to base the new style on an existing style, click the Based On drop-down arrow and select the desired base style from the list.

6. If you want the new style to be part of the template that the current document is based on, select the Add To Template check box. If you do not select this check box, the new style will be available only in the current document.

7. The Automatically Update check box is available only for paragraph styles. If selected, then when you make manual format changes to paragraphs that have this style assigned, the format changes will be added to the style definition.

8. Click the Format button and select Font or Border to specify the font and/or border of the new style. As you make format changes, the Preview box displays an image of what the style will look like, and the Description area provides a description of the style elements.

9. For paragraph styles only, click the Format button and select Paragraph to set the style's indents and line spacing, and select Tabs to set the new style's tab stops.

10. Click OK to return to the Style dialog box.

11. Click Apply to assign the new style to the current text or paragraph. Click Close to save the new style definition without assigning it to any text.

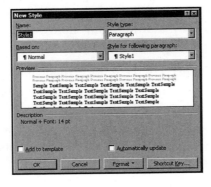

FIGURE 12.3   The New Style dialog box.

MODIFYING A STYLE

You can change the formatting associated with any paragraph or character style, whether it is a style you define or one of Word's predefined styles. When you do so, all text in the document that has the style assigned will be modified. Here's how:

1. Click Format, Style to open the Style dialog box (see Figure 12.4).

2. Click the List drop-down arrow and select which styles should be displayed in the Styles list:

   - All Styles   All styles defined in the current document.

   - Styles in Use   Styles that have been assigned to text in the current document.

   - User Defined Styles   All user-defined styles in the current document.

3. In the Styles list, click the name of the style you want to modify.

4. Click the Modify button. The Modify Style dialog box appears, which looks the same as the New Style dialog box (refer to Figure 12.3). Specify the style's new format specifications.

5. Click OK the return to the Style dialog box, then click Close.

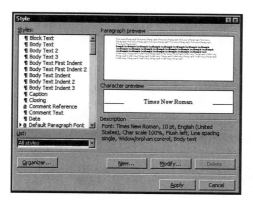

FIGURE 12.4   The Style dialog box.

In this lesson, you learned what styles are, how to apply styles to text, and how to create and modify styles. The next lesson shows you some advanced style techniques.

13 LESSON

ADVANCED STYLE TECHNIQUES

In this lesson, you learn how to assign styles automatically, how to use the heading styles in Outline view, and how to specify spacing between paragraphs. You also learn how to assign shortcut keys to styles and how to find and replace styles.

AUTOMATIC STYLE ASSIGNMENT

When you press Enter to start a new paragraph, Word normally assigns to the new paragraph the same style that is assigned to the first paragraph. There may be times, however, when you want paragraphs of a certain style to always be followed by a differently styled paragraph. For example, say you have created a Section Heading style. Because a section heading is never followed by another section heading, but always by regular text, save yourself time and effort by specifying that paragraphs with the Section Heading style always be followed by a paragraph with the Normal style. Here's how:

1. Click Format, Style to open the Style dialog box. If necessary, select the desired style in the Styles list.

2. Click the Modify button to open the Modify Style dialog box (see Figure 13.1).

3. Click the Style for Following Paragraph drop-down arrow and select the style you want assigned automatically to the following paragraphs.

4. Click OK to return to the Style dialog box, then click Close.

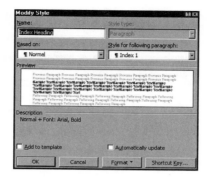

Figure 13.1   The Modify Style dialog box.

When you specify one style to always follow another, it does not affect existing paragraphs in your document. Only new paragraphs are affected as they are added.

USING WORD'S HEADING STYLES IN OUTLINE VIEW

Word's predefined styles include nine heading styles, named Heading 1 through Heading 9; they can be very useful in certain kinds of documents. In addition to being used as regular styles for assigning formatting to text, they are used in Word's Outline view, which you learned about in Lesson 7. In Outline view, each heading style is automatically applied as an outline level, with Heading 1 as the top level, Heading 2 as the next level, and so on. Figure 13.2 shows a document in Outline view with headings displayed.

 TIP   **Outline View**   To switch to Outline view, click the Outline View button or click View, Outline.

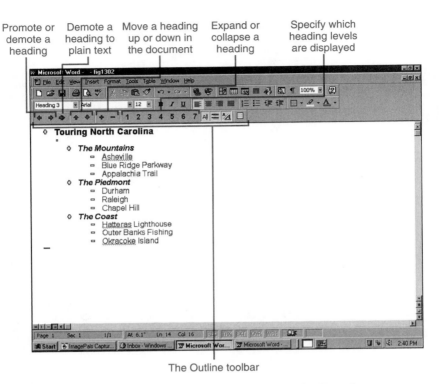

Promote or demote a heading

Demote a heading to plain text

Move a heading up or down in the document

Expand or collapse a heading

Specify which heading levels are displayed

The Outline toolbar

Figure 13.2   A document with headings in Outline view.

In Outline view, you can display headings only for headings and text. When showing headings, you can specify which levels are displayed and which are hidden. You can promote and demote headings, which changes them to a higher or lower heading level. When you promote or demote a heading, all its subheads are promoted or demoted the same number of levels. You can also move headings around in the document, and all the subheadings and text are moved too. You can expand a heading to display the text under it, and then collapse it to hide the text again.

In Outline view, each heading has a plus sign next to it if it has subheadings or text, and a minus sign if it does not. You work with outlines by using these symbols and the Outline toolbar, shown in Figure 13.2. Here are the things you can do in Outline view:

- To promote a heading, drag its symbol to the left, click the Promote button, or press Shift+Tab.

- To demote a heading, drag its symbol to the right, click the Demote button, or press Tab.

- To move a heading to a different location in the document, drags its symbol up or down or click the Move buttons.

- To expand or collapse a heading, click the Expand or Collapse button.

- To control which levels are displayed, click one of the level buttons. For example, click 4 to display levels 1 through 4 and hide lower levels and body text. Click All to display all levels plus body text.

In Outline view, you can edit text, assign styles, and perform other editing tasks in the usual manner. Aside from their use in Outline view, the Heading styles are just like any other style. You can modify the style formatting any way you want.

AUTOMATIC SPACING BETWEEN PARAGRAPHS

The appearance of your documents improves if some blank space is left between the end of one paragraph and the start of the next. You can accomplish this by pressing Enter twice at the end of a paragraph, in effect inserting a blank line between paragraphs. By using styles, you can have greater control over your paragraph spacing and save time, too. Here are the steps:

1. Click Format, Style to open the Style dialog box. Select the paragraph style in the Styles list.

2. Click Modify to open the Modify Style dialog box.

3. Click the Format button, then choose Paragraph from the list that appears. The Paragraph dialog box opens (see Figure 13.3).

4. If necessary, click the Indents and Spacing tab.

5. In the Spacing area, enter the desired spacing or click the incrementer arrows in the Before text box (for space above the paragraph) and/or the After text box (for space below the paragraph).

6. Click OK twice, then click Close. Paragraphs in the selected style will now automatically have the specified amount of blank space above and/or below them.

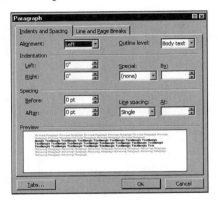

Figure 13.3   The Paragraph dialog box.

The units used to specify the spacing before or after a paragraph are *points*, the same unit that is used to specify font size. Remember, a point is 1/72 of an inch. To have approximately one line of spacing before or after a paragraph, enter a value equal to the point size of the paragraph style's font.

ASSIGNING SHORTCUT KEYS TO STYLES

If you use some styles frequently, or if you prefer using the keyboard to using the mouse, you can assign shortcut key combinations to styles. Then, all you need to do to assign the style is press the specified keys. Here's how to do it:

1. Click Format, Style to open the Style dialog box. Select the desired style in the Styles list.

2. Click Modify to open the Modify Style dialog box.

3. Click the Shortcut Key button to open the Customize Keyboard dialog box (see Figure 13.4).

4. Press the key combination you want assigned to the style. The Press New Shortcut Key box displays a description of the keys you pressed. Just below this box, Word indicates if the shortcut key already has an assigned style/command or if it is unassigned.

5. To accept the shortcut key, click the Assign button. To enter another shortcut key, press Backspace to erase the key, then return to step 4.

6. Click Close to return to the Modify Style dialog box. Click OK to return to the Styles dialog box, and click Close to return to your document.

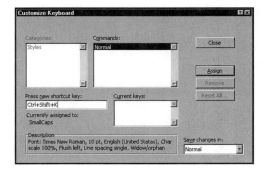

Figure 13.4   The Customize Keyboard dialog box.

You can assign any function (F1-F12) key by itself, but this isn't a good idea because the function keys have Word commands already assigned to them. For example, you can assign the F1 key to a style, but then you will no longer be able to access Help with F1. It is better to use key combinations. Here's what's available:

Ctrl+*key*

Alt+*key*

Ctrl+Alt+*key*

Ctrl+Shift+*key*

Alt+Shift+*key*

Ctrl+Alt+Shift+*key*

For all of the above, *key* can be just about any key on the keyboard. Don't worry about pressing an unacceptable key because if you do, Word won't accept it.

FINDING AND REPLACING STYLES

It's easy enough to change the style of a single paragraph, but what about changing the style of dozens of paragraphs all through the document? For example, you may need to change all paragraphs that have the Normal style to a new style named Fancy1. Or, perhaps you simply need to locate paragraphs that have a particular style assigned. Word's Find and Replace command can help you. Here's how to find paragraphs formatted with a specific style:

1. Click Edit, Find or press Ctrl+F to open the Find tab of the Find and Replace dialog box.

2. Click More to display all of the Find options.

3. Do not enter anything in the Find What text box. Instead, click the Format button then select Style.

4. The Find Style dialog box appears (see Figure 13.5). Select the style you want to find.

5. Click OK to return to the Find dialog box.

6. Click Find Next to begin the search.

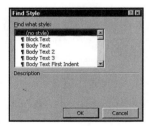

Figure 13.5   The Find Style dialog box.

The following steps show you how to find and replace a style:

1. Click Edit, Replace or press Ctrl+H to open the Replace tab of the Find and Replace dialog box.

2. Click More to display all of the Replace options.

3. Click the Find What text box, but do not enter anything.

4. Click the Format button and select Style to open the Find Style dialog box (refer to Figure 13.5).

5. Select the style you want to replace, then click OK to return to the Find and Replace dialog box.

6. Click the Replace With text box, but again do not enter anything.

7. Click the Format button and select Style to open the Replace Style dialog box.

8. Select the replacement style, then click OK to return to the Find and Replace dialog box.

9. Click the Find Next and Replace buttons to replace the style in individual paragraphs. Click the Replace All button to replace all instances of the first style with the second style.

After using the Find and Replace dialog box to work with styles, click the No Formatting button to remove the formatting specifications and to return to finding or replacing plain text.

In this lesson, you learned how to assign styles automatically, how to use the heading styles in Outline view, and how to specify spacing between paragraphs. You also learned how to assign shortcut keys to styles and how to find and replace styles. The next lesson shows you how to work with margins, pages, and sections.

14 MARGINS, PAGES, AND SECTIONS

In this lesson, you learn how to use document sections, how to set page margins, how to work with different paper sizes, and how to specify the source of paper used in printing.

USING SECTION BREAKS

Word gives you the option of breaking your document into two or more *sections*, each of which can have its own page formatting. You need to use sections only when you want some aspect of page layout, such as page margins (covered later in this lesson) or columns (covered in Lesson 23), to apply to only part of the document. The default is for page layout settings such as these to apply to the entire document.

There are three types of section breaks. They have the same effect in terms of controlling page layout, but differ as to where the text that comes after the break is placed:

- **Next Page**   The new section begins at the top of the next page. This is useful for section breaks that coincide with major breaks in a document, such as a new chapter starting.

- **Continuous**   The new section begins on the same page as the preceding section. This is useful for a section that has a different number of columns from the preceding one but is still part of the same page. An example would be a newsletter; the title runs across the top of the page in one column, and then after a section break, the body of the newsletter appears below the title in three columns.

- **Odd Page or Even Page** The new section begins on the next even- or odd-numbered page. This is useful when a section break coincides with a major break (like a chapter) in a document where each chapter must start on an odd page (or an even page).

In Normal view, Word marks the location of section breaks by displaying a double horizontal line with the label **Section Break** followed by the type of break. These markers do not appear in Page Layout view or in printouts.

To insert a section break:

1. Click Insert, Break to open the Break dialog box.
2. Select the desired type of section break (as described in the previous list).
3. Click OK.

A section break mark is just like any character in your document. To delete a section break, move the cursor right before it and press Delete; or move the cursor right after it and press Backspace. Each section break marker holds the settings for the text that comes before it, so when you delete a section break, text in the section before the break becomes part of the section that was after the break, and it assumes the page layout formatting of that section.

INSERTING MANUAL PAGE BREAKS

When text reaches the bottom margin of a page, Word automatically starts a new page and continues the text at the top of that page. However, you can manually insert page breaks to start a new page at any desired location. Here's how:

1. Click Insert, Break to open the Break dialog box.
2. Select Page Break.
3. Click OK.

Quick Breaks   You can enter a page break by pressing Ctrl+Enter. To start a new line without starting a new paragraph, press Shift+Enter.

A page break appears in the document as a single horizontal line. Like section break markers, page break markers do not appear in Page Layout view or in printouts. To delete a page break, move the cursor to the line containing the break and press Delete.

SETTING PAGE MARGINS

The page margins control the amount of white space between your text and the edges of the page. Each page has four margins: left, right, top, and bottom. When you change page margins, the new settings will affect the entire document or, if you have inserted one or more section breaks, the current section.

The easiest way to set page margins is with your mouse and the Ruler. You can work visually rather than thinking in terms of inches or centimeters. To display the Ruler, click View, Ruler or position the mouse pointer near the top edge of the work area.

You can use the Ruler to change margins only while working in Page Layout view (click View, Page Layout). In Page Layout view, Word displays both a horizontal Ruler at the top of the page and a vertical Ruler on the left edge of the page. This permits you to set both the left/right and the top/bottom margins using a Ruler.

On each Ruler, the white bar shows the current margin settings, as shown in Figure 14.1. To change the left or right margin, point at the margin marker on the horizontal Ruler, at the left or right end of the white bar; the mouse pointer will change to a two-headed arrow. Then, drag the margin to the new position. For the top or bottom margin, follow the same procedure using the vertical Ruler.

Margins   The margins are the distances between the text and the edges of the page.

Left margin line   Top margin line

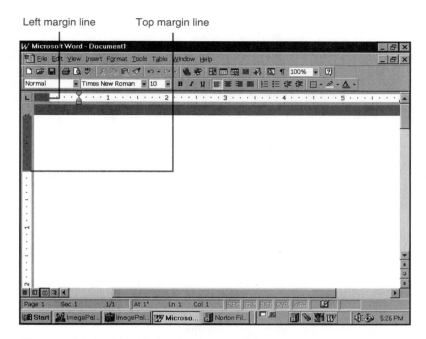

Figure 14.1 The Ruler displays a white bar showing the current margin settings.

Note that the margin symbols on the horizontal Ruler are the vertical edges of the white margin bar, not the small triangular buttons. These buttons are the indent markers, which you learned about in Lesson 10. If your mouse pointer has changed to a two-headed arrow, then you know you have found the margin symbol.

TIP   **Changing Margins**   Margins apply to the entire section, unlike indents (which apply to individual paragraphs). To change the margins for only a portion of a document, insert a section break as described previously in this lesson. You can then specify different margins for each section.

Can't Change Margins?   Be sure you're in Page Layout view or the Rulers won't work for changing margins. (You can, however, drag the indent markers on the ruler in Normal view, as you learned in Lesson 10.)

You can also set the page margins using a dialog box. Use this method when you don't want to use the mouse or need to enter precise margin values. (You also don't have to switch to Page Layout view to do it.) It gives you more control over where in the document the new margins are applied. Here's how:

1. Click File, Page Setup to open the Page Setup dialog box.

2. If necessary, click the Margins tab to display the margins options, as shown in Figure 14.2.

3. In the Top, Bottom, Left, and Right text boxes, enter the desired margin size (in inches) or click the incrementer arrows to set the desired value. The Preview shows you the effects of your margin settings.

4. If your document will be bound and you want to leave an extra large margin on one side for the binding, enter the desired width in the Gutter text box. This extra space will be added to the left margin of every page or, if you select the Mirror Margins check box, it will be added to the left margin of odd-numbered pages and the right margin of even-numbered pages (which is useful for binding a document that is printed on both sides of the paper).

5. Click the Apply To drop-down arrow and select where the new margins will apply from the list. These are your options:

   - **Whole Document**   The new margin settings will apply to the entire document.

   - **This Point Forward**   Word will insert a continuous section break at the cursor location and apply the new margins to the new section.

- **This Section** Margins will be applied to the current document section. This option is not available if you have not broken your document into sections.

6. Click OK.

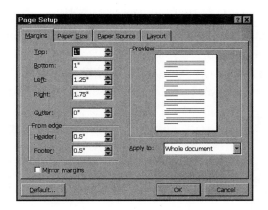

Figure 14.2 Setting margins in the Page Setup dialog box.

CONTROLLING PAPER SIZE AND ORIENTATION

Word's default is to format documents to fit on standard 8-1/2 × 11 inch letter size paper, and to print in portrait orientation, which means the lines of text run parallel to the short edge of the paper. You can specify a different paper size, selecting from several standard paper and envelope sizes or defining a custom paper size. You can also print in landscape orientation, so the lines of text are parallel to the long edge of the paper.

To specify paper size and orientation:

1. Click File, Page Setup to open the Page Setup dialog box.

2. Click the Paper Size tab (see Figure 14.3).

3. Click the Paper Size drop-down arrow and select a pre-defined paper size from the list. Or, enter a custom height and width in the text boxes provided.

4. Select Portrait or Landscape orientation.

5. Click the Apply To drop-down arrow and select the portion of the document that the new paper setting is to apply:

   - **Whole Document**   The new paper setting will be used for the entire document.

   - **This Point Forward**   Word will insert a continuous section break at the cursor location and apply the new paper settings to the new section.

   - **This Section**   Paper settings will be applied to the current document section. This option is not available if your document has not been broken into sections.

6. Select OK.

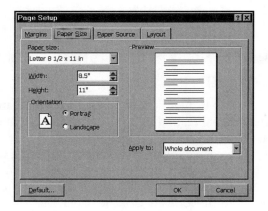

Figure 14.3   Setting paper size and orientation.

Specifying a Paper Source

Some documents require printing on different kinds of paper. For example, with a multi-page business letter you may want to print the first page on company letterhead and the other pages on plain paper. Within the limitations of your printer, you can tell Word where it should get the paper for each section of the document. Most laser printers give you two choices: the regular paper tray or manual feed. Advanced printers will have more options, such as two or more paper trays and an envelope feeder.

To specify the paper source:

1. Click File, Page Setup to open the Page Setup dialog box.

2. Click the Paper Source tab (see Figure 14.4).

3. In the First Page list box, specify the paper source for the first page. The choices available here will depend on your printer model.

4. In the Other Pages list box, specify the paper source for the second and subsequent pages.

5. Click the Apply To drop-down arrow and select which part of the document the paper source settings should apply to.

6. Select OK.

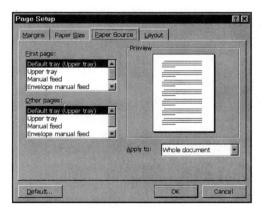

Figure 14.4 Specifying the paper source.

In this lesson, you learned how to use document sections, how to set page margins, how to work with different paper sizes, and how to specify the source of paper used in printing. In the next lesson, you will learn how to use Word's AutoText and AutoCorrect features.

LESSON 15

USING AUTOCORRECT AND AUTOTEXT

In this lesson, you learn how to use Word's AutoText and AutoCorrect features.

WHAT DO AUTOCORRECT AND AUTOTEXT DO?

AutoCorrect and AutoText are very useful features that can save you a lot of time. They're related to each other, but each one has a different purpose:

- AutoCorrect looks for common typing and spelling mistakes in your document, and automatically corrects them as they happen. For example, you could tell AutoCorrect to always replace "teh" with "the."

- AutoText lets you define and store frequently used sections of text and/or graphics, and then insert them in the document as needed. For example, you could define an AutoText entry containing your complete name and address then insert it with a few keystrokes.

 Where's My Glossary? In previous versions of Word, the AutoText feature was called the Glossary.

DEFINING AN AUTOCORRECT ENTRY

There are two parts to AutoCorrect. One part deals with capitalization errors, such as forgetting to capitalize the first letter of a sentence. The other deals with spelling errors and the addition of special symbols. Thus, AutoCorrect can automatically replace "acn" with "can" and it can replace "—>" with an arrow symbol. Word has a number of default AutoCorrect entries, and you can create your own.

AutoCorrect text can be plain text that will take on the paragraph formatting at the location where it is inserted, or it can be formatted text that retains its original formatting. Here's how to create AutoCorrect entries:

1. If you want formatting to accompany the text, you must select the formatted text in the document. If you want the entry to be inserted as a separate paragraph, be sure to select the paragraph mark at the end of the text. To create a plain text AutoCorrect entry, selecting text is optional.

2. Click Tools, AutoCorrect to open the AutoCorrect dialog box (see Figure 15.1).

3. Type the text to be replaced in the Replace text box. This is the text that will be replaced when you type it in the document.

4. If you selected document text in step 1, it will already be entered in the With text box. Otherwise, type the desired replacement text in the With text box.

5. Select the Formatted Text option if you want the text's formatting to be inserted as well. Select the Plain Text option to insert the text without formatting.

6. Click the Add button. If the replacement text you specified is already defined in the AutoCorrect list, Word asks if you want to redefine it. If not, select No to return to step 3. Otherwise select Yes.

7. Click OK.

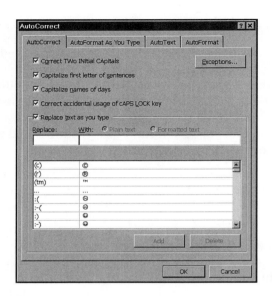

Figure 15.1　The AutoCorrect dialog box.

While you are editing a document, AutoCorrect checks complete words only. Thus, if you type "teh" Word will not replace it with "the" until you press spacebar, period, or some other key indicating the end of the word.

Bad Speller?　Define AutoCorrect entries for the words you commonly misspell, and you won't have to spend time correcting them.

MODIFYING AUTOCORRECT SETTINGS

You can modify the AutoCorrect settings so it works the way you want. Here are the steps to follow:

1. Click Tools, AutoCorrect to open the AutoCorrect dialog box (refer to Figure 15.1).

2. Do any of the following:

- To control the way AutoCorrect deals with capitalization errors, select or deselect the four check boxes at the top of the dialog box.

- To enable or disable automatic text replacement, select or deselect the Replace Text as You Type check box.

- To delete an AutoCorrect entry, select it in the list and click Delete.

- To modify an entry, select it in the list, edit the text in the With text box, and select Replace.

3. Click OK.

Word also lets you customize the way that AutoCorrect's Correct Two Initial Capitals and Capitalize First Letter of Sentences features operate:

- Certain acronyms or other abbreviations may properly have two initial capitals; you can specify that AutoCorrect ignore them.

- Word capitalizes the first letter of a sentence based on the end of the previous sentence as marked by a period or other character. If, however, a sentence contains an abbreviation with a period (such as "acct."), you will not want the next word capitalized. Word has a default list of abbreviations to be ignored; you can modify this list as needed.

Here's how to customize AutoCorrect's capitalization settings:

1. Click Tools, AutoCorrect to open the AutoCorrect dialog box.

2. Click the Exceptions button to open the AutoCorrect Exceptions dialog box.

3. Click the INitial Caps tab, then enter the acronym to be ignored in the Don't Correct text box and select Add. Select an acronym in the list and click Delete to remove it.

4. Click the First Letter tab and enter the abbreviation to be ignored in the Don't Capitalize After text box, then select Add. Select an abbreviation in the list and click Delete to remove it.

5. Select OK to return to the AutoCorrect dialog box.

Note that AutoCorrect works only on text you type. For example, if you open a document that was created by someone else, AutoCorrect will not correct errors in the document.

CREATING AUTOTEXT DEFINITIONS

Word lets you store any text and graphics in a named AutoText entry. Then, you can insert the text or graphics in any document simply by typing or selecting its name.

When you create an AutoText entry, it is linked to the paragraph style of the original text from which the entry was created. When you need to insert an AutoText entry, the list will display only those entries associated with the current paragraph style. The exception is the Normal paragraph style, for which all entries are always available. Thus, if you create an AutoText entry from text in a paragraph formatted with a style named Formal, that AutoText entry will be available only when the cursor is in a paragraph that also has the style Formal applied to it.

TIP   **The AutoText Toolbar**   If you use AutoText frequently, you may find it convenient to have the AutoText toolbar displayed. Select View, Toolbars then select AutoText.

To create an AutoText entry:

1. Select the text and/or graphics to be in the entry. If you want the text's formatting included as part of the entry, be sure to include the paragraph marker in the selection.

2. Press Alt+F3; click the New button on the AutoText toolbar; or select Insert, AutoText, New. The Create AutoText dialog box appears (see Figure 15.2).

3. You can accept the AutoText name that Word suggests, or enter your own in the box.

4. Select OK.

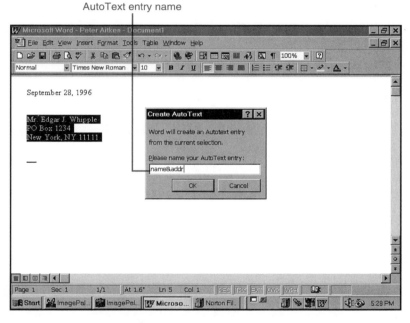

Figure 15.2   Creating a new AutoText entry.

INSERTING AUTOTEXT

There are several methods available for inserting AutoText entries:

- If the AutoText toolbar is displayed, click the middle button. This button is labeled with the name of the current paragraph style, or if the current style is Normal it is labeled **All Entries**. Then select the desired AutoText entry from the list.

- If AutoComplete is enabled (see the following steps), start typing the name of the AutoText entry. When you have typed enough of the name to identify the entry, Word displays the matching AutoText entry in a small "tip" box next to the cursor, as shown in Figure 15.3. To insert the entire entry, press F3 or Enter. To ignore it, simply keep typing.

- Select Insert, AutoText, then select the desired entry from the submenu.

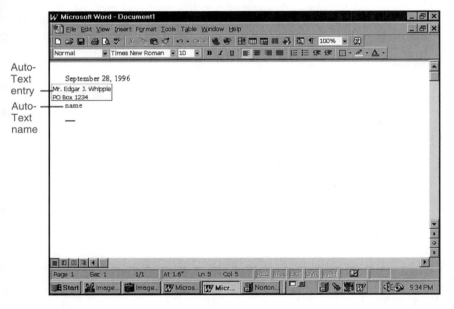

Figure 15.3 Using AutoComplete to insert an AutoText entry.

If the current paragraph has been assigned a paragraph style other than Normal, the AutoText list will display only those entries that have been associated with that style. To display all AutoText entries in this situation, hold down the Shift key while clicking the

AutoText toolbar or when selecting AutoText from the Insert menu.

The AutoComplete option is controlled from the AutoText tab of the AutoCorrect dialog box. You also use this tab to delete AutoText entries. Here are the steps to follow:

1. Select Insert, AutoText, AutoText or click the button at the left end of the AutoText toolbar to open the AutoText dialog box (see Figure 15.4).

2. Select or deselect the Show AutoComplete Tip for AutoText and Dates check box.

3. To delete an AutoText entry, select it in the list and click Delete.

4. Select OK.

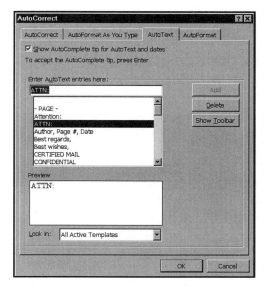

Figure 15.4   The AutoText tab.

AUTOCORRECT VERSUS AUTOTEXT

You may have realized that you can use AutoCorrect to perform the task of AutoText, at least for inserting text. (AutoCorrect cannot insert graphics.) Thus, if your name is Heironymous J. Whipplesnapper, you could define an AutoCorrect entry "hjw" to automatically insert your name. The major difference is that AutoCorrect entries are inserted automatically, whereas AutoText entries require user confirmation.

This lesson showed you how to use Word's AutoText and AutoCorrect features. The next lesson covers automatic formatting.

APPLYING AUTOMATIC FORMATTING

In this lesson, you learn how to use Word's automatic formatting capability.

WHAT AUTOFORMATTING CAN DO

Automatic formatting is Word's capability to analyze the parts of a document and recognize certain elements, such as body text, headings, bulleted lists, and quotations. Word will then apply appropriate styles to the various text elements to create an attractively formatted document. (You learned about styles in Lessons 12 and 13.) You can accept or reject the automatically applied format, in part or in whole, and can later make any desired modifications to the document.

In addition to applying styles, automatic formatting removes extra "returns" between paragraphs; automatically formats Internet, network, and e-mail addresses as hyperlinks; applies bold or underline character formatting to text surrounded by asterisks (*) or underscores (_); replaces two hyphens (--) with an em dash (—) and more.

TIP   **Word on the Web**   If you format Internet and e-mail addresses as hyperlinks, users will be able to access them over the Internet simply by clicking the link in the document.

There are two ways to use automatic formatting: Word can format items as you type them, or you can create an unformatted document and then apply automatic formatting to the entire document.

Is automatic formatting right for you? The only way to find out is to try it for yourself. Take a document that characterizes the ones you usually work on, save it under a new name (so the original is not changed) and experiment. You'll soon find out whether you like automatic formatting, or whether you prefer manually formatting your documents.

 Try It Out   You should give automatic formatting a try. If you like the results, it can save you a lot of time.

Applying Formatting as You Type

Word can apply a variety of formatting to text as you type it. Some examples are:

- **Tables**   If you type a line of plus signs and hyphens (such as + -- + -- +), and then press Enter, Word creates a table with one column for each pair of plus signs. The table will initially have one row, and the cursor will be positioned in the first cell.

- **Borders**   If you type three or more hyphens, underscores, or equal signs, Word will insert a thin, thick, or double border, respectively.

- **Bulleted Lists**   If you start a paragraph with an asterisk, a lower case "o", or a hyphen, and then type a space or tab, Word automatically creates a bulleted list.

To control the formatting that is applied as you type:

1. Select Format, AutoFormat to display the AutoFormat dialog box.

2. Click the Options button to open the AutoCorrect dialog box.

3. Click the AutoFormat As You Type tab to see the options shown in Figure 16.1.

4. Select or deselect the check boxes as desired.

 What's That Do?   Remember, you can get Help information on any option by clicking the AutoHelp button (the question mark) of a dialog box's title bar then clicking the option.

5. Select OK.

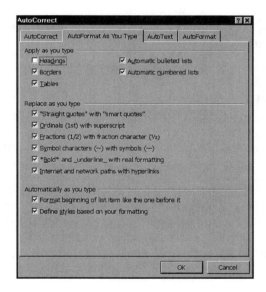

FIGURE 16.1   Setting the AutoFormat As You Type options.

Changing options in this dialog box does not affect text that has already been formatted. It affects only text that is typed after the options are changed.

APPLYING AUTOFORMATTING TO YOUR DOCUMENT

Here are the steps required to apply automatic formatting to the entire document:

1. Select Format, AutoFormat to open the AutoFormat dialog box.

2. Select AutoFormat Now to apply AutoFormatting without reviewing individual changes. Select AutoFormat and Review Each Change if you want to be able to accept or reject each format change.

3. (Optional) Click the Document Type drop-down arrow and select the type of document you are working on from the list.

4. Select OK.

If you selected AutoFormat Now in step 2, Word analyzes your document and applies formatting based on the document contents. You cannot reverse individual formatting changes, but you can undo the entire AutoFormat effect by selecting Edit, Undo AutoFormat.

If you selected AutoFormat and Review Each Change in step 2, Word formats your document and displays the AutoFormat dialog box shown in Figure 16.2. You can scroll around in your document while this dialog box is displayed to view the changes that Word made. Then, make choices in this dialog box as follows:

- Accept All   Accepts all formatting changes.

- Reject All   Rejects all formatting changes.

- Review Changes   Lets you view each formatting change and accept or reject it (see the next paragraph).

- Style Gallery   Displays the Style Gallery from which you can select an overall "look" for your document. After you select a style, you return to the AutoFormat dialog box.

FIGURE 16.2   The AutoFormat dialog box.

If you decide to review changes, the Review AutoFormat Changes
dialog box appears (see Figure 16.3). You use the commands in
this dialog box to examine the format changes one at a time,
accepting or rejecting each one. Font changes are not reviewed,
but all other formatting changes are. While you are working in
this dialog box, Word displays the document with marks
indicating the changes made, as described in Table 16.1.

**TABLE 16.1 MARKS DISPLAYED TO INDICATE AUTOFORMAT
CHANGES**

CHANGE MADE	MARK DISPLAYED
New style applied to the paragraph	Blue paragraph mark
Paragraph mark deleted	Red paragraph mark
Text or spaces deleted	Strikethrough
Characters added	Underline
Text or formatting changed	Vertical bar in left margin

FIGURE 16.3   The Review AutoFormat Changes dialog box.

Table 16.2 describes the actions you can take in the Review Auto Format dialog box.

TABLE 16.2   COMMANDS USED WHILE REVIEWING AUTOFORMAT CHANGES

BUTTON	ACTION
⇐ Find	Locates and highlights the previous change.
⇒ Find	Locates and highlights the next change.
Reject	Undoes the current formatting change.
Hide Marks	Hides the marks in the document to make it easier to evaluate its appearance. Click Show Marks to redisplay the marks.
Undo	Reinstates a rejected change.
Cancel	Returns to the AutoFormat dialog box.

Note that you do not need to take any action to accept a change. Changes you do not explicitly reject are automatically accepted.

 Oops! To be sure you can recover from unwanted AutoFormat changes, first save your document under a different name.

SETTING AUTOFORMAT OPTIONS

The AutoFormat feature has a number of settings that control which document elements it will modify. You can change these options to suit your preferences:

1. Select Format, AutoFormat to open the AutoFormat dialog box.

2. Click the Options button to open the AutoCorrect dialog box.

3. Click the AutoFormat tab to display the AutoFormat options (see Figure 16.4).

4. Select or deselect the various AutoFormat check boxes as desired. Use AutoHelp as needed (click the question mark in the dialog box's title bar, then click on the element you need help with) to get information on individual options.

5. Select OK.

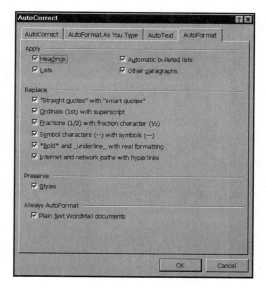

FIGURE 16.4   Setting AutoFormat options.

Changes you make to AutoFormat options will not affect a previously formatted document, but will apply to future uses of the AutoFormat command.

In this lesson, you learned how to use Word's AutoFormat command. The next lesson teaches you how to work with document templates.

17

WORKING WITH TEMPLATES

In this lesson, you learn how to create new document templates and how to modify existing templates.

CREATING A NEW TEMPLATE

You learned in Lesson 4 that every Word document is based on a template, and that Word comes with a variety of predefined templates. You can also create your own templates, or modify existing templates, to suit your individual needs.

You can create a new template based on an existing template, and the new template will contain all the elements of the base template plus any text or formatting you add. To create a new template from scratch, base it on the Blank Document template. Here are the steps to follow:

1. Select File, New to open the New dialog box (see Figure 17.1).

2. Click the Template option button.

3. If you want the new template based on an existing template, select that template icon in the dialog box. Otherwise, select the Blank Document icon.

4. Select OK. A blank document-editing screen appears with a default name, such as TEMPLATE1.

5. Enter the boilerplate text and other items that you want to be part of the new template, and apply formatting to the text as desired. You should also create any styles that you want in the template.

6. Select File, Save or click the Save button on the Standard toolbar. The Save As dialog box appears.

7. If necessary, select the folder you want the new template saved in by double-clicking its name. For example, if it is a template for a letter, you would probably save it in the Letters & Faxes folder.

8. In the File Name text box, enter a descriptive name up to 256 characters long for the template. Be sure to use a different name from the template you selected in step 3, or the new template will replace the original one.

9. Select Save. The template is saved under the specified name and is now available for use each time you start a new document.

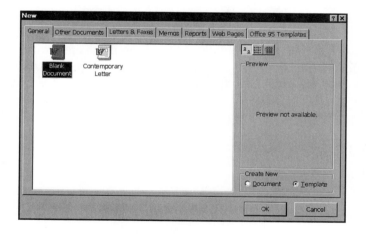

FIGURE 17.1   Creating a new template based on the Blank Document template.

Boilerplate   This is text that you want to appear in every document based on the new template.

MODIFYING AN EXISTING TEMPLATE

You can retrieve any existing template from disk and modify it. Here's how:

1. Select File, New to open the New dialog box.

2. Select the tab containing the template you want to modify, then select the template icon you want to modify.

3. Select the Template option button.

4. Click OK.

5. Make the desired modifications and additions to the template's text and styles.

 6. Select File, Save or click the Save button on the Standard toolbar. The modified template will be saved to disk.

When you modify a template, changes you make are not reflected in documents that were created based on the template before it was changed. Only new documents will be affected.

 Save the Old   Rather than modifying a template, it's often better to create a new template based on it. This way the original template will still be available should you change your mind.

 Recycle Old Templates?   You can use old templates from earlier versions of Word (Word for Windows 95 and Word for Windows 6.0) to create new documents in Word.

CREATING A TEMPLATE FROM A DOCUMENT

Sometimes you will find it useful to create a template based on an existing Word document. Here are the steps to follow:

1. Open the document that you want to base the new template on.

2. Use Word's editing commands to delete any document text and formatting that you do not want to appear in the template.

3. Select File, Save As to open the Save As dialog box (see Figure 17.2).

4. Click the Save as Type drop-down arrow and choose Document Template from the list. The Save In box automatically changes to indicate the Templates folder.

5. If appropriate, select the folder where you want the template saved by double-clicking its name.

6. Type a descriptive name for the template in the File Name text box.

7. Select Save.

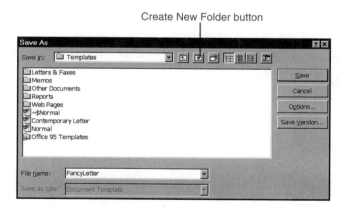

Create New Folder button

FIGURE 17.2 Saving a document template.

In step 5, it's important to select the proper template folder. When you select Document Template in step 4, Word automatically switches to the Templates folder (which is different from where documents are saved). Templates saved in this folder will appear on the General tab in the New dialog box. Because

Word organizes templates by category, you may want to place your new template in the appropriate folder or you may have trouble finding it later. For example, if you create a template for a memo, save it in the Memos folder and it will appear on the Memos tab in the New dialog box.

 No Folder?   If there is not an appropriate folder for your new template, create a new folder by clicking the Create New Folder button in the Save As dialog box.

UPDATING A DOCUMENT WHEN THE TEMPLATE CHANGES

If you modify a template, only new documents based on that template will reflect the changes. Existing documents that were based on the old version of the template will not be affected. You can, however, import new styles from a modified template to an existing document. Here's how:

1. Open the document.

2. Select Tools, Templates and Add-ins.

3. Select the Automatically Update Document Styles check box.

4. Select OK.

With this check box selected, the document styles will automatically be updated to reflect the styles in its attached template each time the document is loaded. Other elements of a template, such as boilerplate text, will not be affected.

In this lesson, you learned how to create and modify document templates. The next lesson shows you how to use page numbers, headers, and footers in your documents.

PAGE NUMBERS, HEADERS, AND FOOTERS

In this lesson, you learn how to add page numbers, headers, and footers to your documents.

ADDING PAGE NUMBERS

Many documents, particularly long ones, require that the pages be numbered. Word offers many choices as to the placement and appearance of page numbers. Page numbers are always part of a header or footer. You can place a page number by itself in a header or footer, as covered in this section. You can also include additional information in the header or footer, as covered later in this lesson. To add page numbers to your document:

1. Select Insert, Page Numbers. The Page Numbers dialog box appears, as shown in Figure 18.1.

2. Click the Position drop-down arrow and select the desired position on the page: Top of Page (Header) or Bottom of Page (Footer).

3. Click the Alignment drop-down arrow and select Left, Center, or Right. You can also select Inside or Outside if you're printing two-sided pages and want the page numbers positioned near to (Inside) or away from (Outside) the binding.

4. The default number format consists of Arabic numerals (1, 2, 3, and so on). To select a different format (such as, i, ii, iii), click Format and select the desired format.

5. Select OK.

Figure 18.1   The Page Numbers dialog box.

Two-sided printing is an option on certain printers. Lesson 14 shows you how to set margins for two sided printing.

When you add a page number using this procedure, Word makes the page number part of the document's header or footer. The next section describes headers and footers.

No Page Numbers Command?   When you're in Online Layout view or Outline view, the Page Numbers option is not available on the Insert menu. In Normal view, you can add—but not see—page numbers.

What Are Headers and Footers?

A *header* or *footer* is text that prints at the top (a header) or bottom (a footer) of every page of a document. A header or footer can show the page number and are useful for displaying chapter titles, authors' names, and similar information. Word offers several header/footer options, including the following:

- The same header/footer on every page of the document.

- One header/footer on the first page of the document and a different header/footer on all other pages.

- One header/footer on odd-numbered pages and a different header/footer on even-numbered pages.

- If your document is divided into sections, you can have a different header/footer for each section.

Headers and Footers   Text that is displayed at the top (header) or bottom (footer) of every page.

ADDING OR EDITING A HEADER OR FOOTER

To add a header or footer to your document, or to edit an existing header or footer, follow these steps:

1. If your document is divided into sections, move the cursor to any location in the section where you want the header or footer placed.

 2. Select View, Header and Footer. Word switches to Page Layout view and displays the current page's header enclosed in a nonprinting dashed line (see Figure 18.2). Regular document text is dimmed, and the Header and Footer toolbar is displayed. On the toolbar, click the Switch button to switch between the current page's header and footer.

3. Enter the header or footer text and formatting using the normal Word editing techniques. Use the Alignment buttons on the Formatting toolbar to control the placement of items in the header/footer.

4. Use the other toolbar buttons, which are described in Table 18.1, to perform the indicated actions.

5. When finished, click the Close button on the Header and Footer toolbar to return to the document.

 Good-bye, Header!   To delete the contents of a header or footer, follow the previous steps for editing the header or footer. Select all of the text in the header or footer; press Delete.

TABLE 18.1   HEADER AND FOOTER TOOLBAR BUTTONS

BUTTON	DESCRIPTION
Insert AutoText ▾	Inserts an AutoText entry (see Lesson 15)
#	Inserts a page number code
⊞	Inserts the total number of pages
#	Formats the page number
📅	Inserts a date code
🕐	Inserts a time code
📖	Opens the Page Setup dialog box so you can set margins (Lesson 14)
▤	Shows or hides document text
▤▤	Makes the header/footer the same as the previous one
▤	Switches between header and footer
◄▤	Shows the previous header or footer
▤►	Shows the next header or footer
Close	Close the Header and Footer toolbar and return to the document

Header box   A page number   Header and Footer toolbar

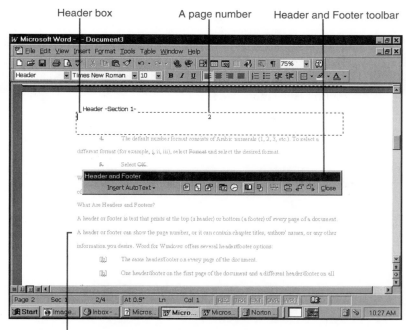

Document text is grayed out

FIGURE 18.2   The Header and Footer toolbar.

CREATING DIFFERENT HEADERS AND FOOTERS FOR DIFFERENT PAGES

Word's default is to display the same header/footer on all the pages in a section or document. One way to have different headers/footers in different parts of the document is to break the document into two or more sections, as explained in Lesson 14. Then, you can use the techniques described earlier in the lesson to add a different header/footer to each section.

In addition to using sections, you have the following options:

- One header/footer on the first page with a different header/footer on all other pages.

- One header/footer on odd-numbered pages with another header/footer on even-numbered pages.

To activate one or both of these options:

1. Select View, Header and Footer.

2. Click the Page Setup button on the Header and Footer toolbar. Word displays the Layout tab of the Page Setup dialog box (see Figure 18.3).

3. Select the Different Odd and Even check box and/or the Different First Page check box.

4. Select OK to close the Page Setup dialog box.

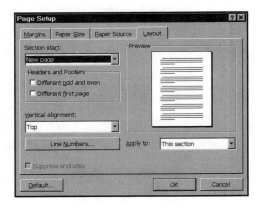

FIGURE 18.3   Setting header/footer options in the Page Setup dialog box.

After selecting one of these header/footer options, use the techniques described earlier in this lesson to add and edit the header/footer text. For example, say you specified Different Odd and Even. If the cursor is on an even-numbered page, you can edit the header/footer text that will display on even-numbered pages. If you click the Show Next button on the Header/Footer toolbar, you move to the header/footer for odd-numbered pages.

In this lesson, you learned to add page numbers, headers, and footers to a document. In the next lesson, you learn how to create numbered and bulleted lists.

NUMBERED AND BULLETED LISTS

This lesson shows you how to add numbered and bulleted lists to your documents.

WHY USE NUMBERED AND BULLETED LISTS?

Numbered and bulleted lists are useful formatting tools for setting off lists of information in a document—you've seen plenty of both in this book! Word can automatically create both types of lists. Use bulleted lists for items that consist of related information, but are in no particular order. Use numbered lists for items with a specific order. When you create a numbered or bulleted list, each paragraph is considered a separate list item and receives its own number or bullet.

CREATING A NUMBERED OR BULLETED LIST

You can create a list from existing text or create the list as you type. To create a numbered or bulleted list from existing text, follow these steps:

1. Select the paragraphs you want in the list.

2. Select Format, Bullets and Numbering to open the Bullets and Numbering dialog box.

3. Depending on the type of list you want, click the Bulleted tab or the Numbered tab. Figure 19.1 shows the Numbered tab options, and Figure 19.2 shows the Bulleted tab options.

4. Click the bullet or number style you want.

5. Select OK.

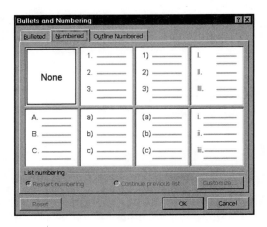

Figure 19.1 Numbered list style options in the Numbered tab.

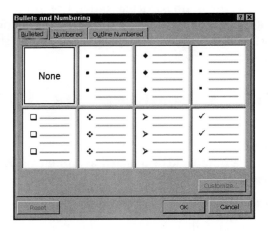

Figure 19.2 Bulleted list style options in the Bulleted tab.

To create a numbered or bulleted list as you type:

1. Move the insertion point to the location for the list. Press Enter, if necessary, to start a new paragraph.

2. Select Format, Bullets and Numbering to open the Bullets and Numbering dialog box.

3. Depending on the type of list you want, click the Bulleted tab or the Numbered tab.

4. Click the bullet or number style you want.

5. Select OK.

6. Type the list elements, pressing Enter at the end of each paragraph. Each new paragraph will automatically be numbered or bulleted as it is added.

7. At the end of the last paragraph, press Enter twice.

 TIP **Quick Lists** Quickly create a numbered or bulleted list in the default list style by clicking the Numbering or Bullets button on the Formatting toolbar before typing or after selecting the list text.

 TIP **Automatic Lists** If the corresponding AutoFormat options are on, Word will automatically start a numbered or bulleted list if you start a paragraph with a number and period or an asterisk followed by a space or tab. To turn these options on or off, select Format, AutoFormat, Options and turn the Lists and the Automatic Bulleted Lists check boxes on or off.

USING MULTILEVEL LISTS

A multilevel list contains two or more levels of bullets or numbering within a single list. For example, a numbered list could contain a lettered list under each numbered item, or each level could be numbered separately, as in an outline. Here's how to create a multilevel list:

1. Select Format, Bullets and Numbering to open the Bullets and Numbering dialog box.

2. Click the Outline Numbered tab to display the multilevel options, as shown in Figure 19.3.

3. Click the list style you want, then click OK.

4. Start typing the list, pressing Enter after each item.

5. After pressing Enter, press Tab to demote the new item one level, or Shift+Tab to promote it one level. Otherwise, the new item will be at the same level as the previous item.

 6. After typing the last item, press Enter, and then click the Numbering button on the Formatting toolbar to end the list.

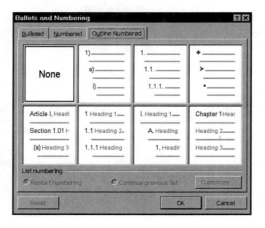

Figure 19.3   Use the Outline Numbered tab of the Bullets and Numbering dialog box to create a multilevel list.

You can convert regular text or a one level numbered or bulleted list to a multilevel list. You can also change the style of an existing multilevel list. Here are the steps to follow:

1. Select all the paragraphs to be in the new list or whose format you want to modify.

2. Select Format, Bullets and Numbering, then click the Outline Numbered tab.

3. Click the desired list style, then click OK.

4. Move the insertion point to an item in the list whose level you want to change.

5. Click the Decrease Indent or Increase Indent buttons on the Formatting toolbar to change the item's level.

6. Repeat steps 4 and 5 as needed to change other items.

REMOVING A NUMBERED OR BULLETED LIST

Follow these steps to remove bullets or numbers from a list while keeping the text and converting it to normal paragraphs:

1. Select the paragraphs from which you want the bullets or numbering removed. This can be the entire list or just part of it. The corresponding button (Bullets or Numbering) on the Formatting toolbar will appear depressed.

2. Click the Bullets or Numbering button.

CHANGING THE FORMAT OF A NUMBERED OR BULLETED LIST

You can also change the format of an existing bulleted or numbered list, to change the bullet symbol or the numbering style:

1. Select the paragraphs from which you want the bullets or numbering removed. This can be the entire list or just part of it.

2. Select Format, Bullets and Numbering to open the Bullets and Numbering dialog box.

3. For a bulleted list, click the Bulleted tab and select the

desired style. Select None to remove bullets.

4. For a numbered list, click the Numbered tab and select the desired numbering style, or click None to remove numbering from the list.

5. Select OK.

Adding Items to Numbered and Bulleted Lists

You can add new items to a numbered or bulleted list as follows:

1. Move the insertion point to the location in the list where you want the new item.

2. Press Enter to start a new paragraph. Word automatically inserts a new bullet or number, and renumbers the list items as needed.

3. Type the new text.

4. If it's a multilevel list, click the Decrease Indent and Increase Indent buttons on the Formatting toolbar to change the item's level, if desired.

5. Repeat as many times as needed.

This lesson showed you how to create numbered and bulleted lists. The next lesson shows you how to add symbols and other special characters to your document.

USING SYMBOLS AND SPECIAL CHARACTERS

In this lesson, you learn how to use symbols and special characters.

WHAT ARE SYMBOLS AND SPECIAL CHARACTERS?

Symbols and *special characters* are not part of the standard character set, and therefore will not be found on your keyboard. Accented letters (such as é), the Greek letter mu (μ), and the copyright symbol (©) are examples. Even though these characters are not on your keyboard, Word can still insert them in your documents.

INSERTING A SYMBOL

To insert a symbol in your document, follow these steps:

1. Select Insert, Symbol to open the Symbol dialog box (see Figure 20.1). Click the Symbols tab if it is not already displayed.

2. Click the Font drop-down arrow and select the desired symbol set from the list. The ones you will use most often are:

   - **Symbol** Greek letters, mathematical symbols, arrows, trademark and copyright symbols, and more.

   - **Normal Text** Letters with accents and other special marks, currency symbols, the paragraph symbol, and more.

- **WindDings**   Icons for clocks, envelopes, telephones, and so on.

3. Look through the grid of symbols for the one you want. To see an enlarged view of a symbol, click it.

4. To insert a highlighted symbol, select Insert. To insert any symbol, double-click it.

5. Click the Cancel button to close the dialog box without inserting a symbol. Click Close to close the dialog box after you insert one or more symbols.

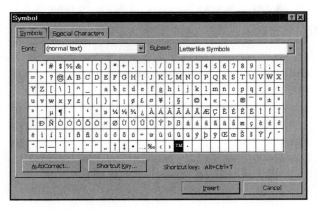

FIGURE 20.1   The Symbol dialog box.

INSERTING A SPECIAL CHARACTER

The distinction between "special characters" and "symbols" is not a clear one. In fact, there is some overlap between the two. Symbols include letters with accents and other diacritical marks used in some languages, Greek letters, arrows, and mathematical symbols (such as ±). Special characters include the copyright symbol (©), ellipses (...), and typographic symbols such as em spaces (a wider than normal space). You'll see that Word provides many more symbols than special characters. To insert a special character in your document:

1. Select Insert, Symbol to open the Symbol dialog box.

2. Click the Special Characters tab to display the special characters list, as shown in Figure 20.2.

3. Look through the list of special characters for the one you want.

4. To insert a highlighted character, select Insert. To insert any character in the list, double-click it.

5. Click the Cancel button to close the dialog box without inserting a character. Click Close to close the dialog box after you insert a character.

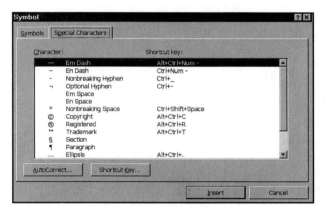

FIGURE 20.2   The Special Characters list.

ASSIGNING SHORTCUT KEYS TO SYMBOLS

You may want to assign shortcut keys to symbols you use frequently. Then you can insert it quickly by pressing that key combination. Most of the special characters already have shortcut keys assigned to them; you can view these key assignments in the Special Character tab in the Symbol dialog box.

TIP   **More Shortcuts**   You can also use Word's AutoCorrect feature to quickly insert symbols and special characters. See Lesson 15 for more information.

To assign a shortcut key to a symbol:

1. Select Insert, Symbol, and click the Symbols tab (refer to Figure 20.1).

2. Click the desired symbol. If necessary, first select the proper font from the Font list.

3. If the selected symbol already has a shortcut key assigned to it, the key description displays in the lower-right corner of the dialog box.

4. Click the Shortcut Key button to display the Customize Keyboard dialog box (see Figure 20.3).

5. Press Alt+N to move to the Press New Shortcut Key text box (or click in the box).

6. Press the shortcut key combination you want to assign. Its description appears in the Press New ShortCut Key text box. A list of permitted key combinations follows these steps.

7. If the specified key combination is unassigned, Word displays **[unassigned]** under the Press New Shortcut Key text box. If it has already been assigned, Word displays the name of the symbol, macro, or command that the selected shortcut key is assigned to.

8. If the shortcut key is unassigned, click Assign to assign it to the symbol. If it is already assigned, press Backspace to delete the shortcut key display and return to step 6 to try another key combination.

9. When done, select Close to return to the Symbols dialog box, and select Close again to return to your document.

The shortcut keys are really key combinations; you can select from the following (where *key* is a letter key, number key, function key, or cursor movement key):

Shift+*key*

Ctrl+*key*

Alt+*key*

Alt+Ctrl+*key*

Alt+Shift+*key*

Ctrl+Shift+*key*

Ctrl+Shift+Alt+*key*

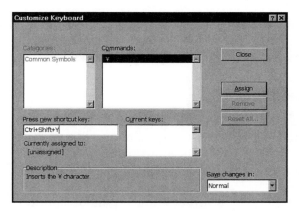

FIGURE 20.3   Assigning a shortcut key to a symbol.

UNDERSTANDING SPECIAL CHARACTERS

Some of the special characters that Word offers may seem unfamiliar to you, but they can be quite useful in certain documents. The following are brief descriptions of the less well-known ones:

- **En dash**   A dash that is the same as the standard dash (inserted with the key above the P key on your keyboard). The en dash is properly used in combinations of figures and/or capital letters, as in "Please refer to part 1–A."

- **Em dash**   Slightly longer than an en dash, the em dash has a variety of purposes, the most common of which is to mark a sudden change of thought. For example, "She said—and no one dared disagree—that the meeting was over."

- **En space**   A space slightly longer than the standard space. This space is an en space.

- **Em space**   A space slightly longer than the en space. This space   is an em space.

- **Non-breaking space**   A space that will not be broken at the end of the line. The words separated by a non-breaking space always stay on the same line.

- **Non-breaking hyphen**   Similar to a non-breaking space. That is to say, two words separated by a non-breaking hyphen will always stay on the same line.

- **Optional hyphen**   A hyphen that will not display unless the word it is in needs to be broken at the end of a line.

In this lesson, you learned how to use symbols and special characters in your Word documents. In the next lesson, you will learn how to proof your document.

Proofing Your Document

This lesson shows you how to use Word's spelling and grammar checker, thesaurus, and Print Preview window to proof your document.

Using the Spelling Checker

Word's spelling checker lets you verify and correct the spelling of words in your document. Words are checked against a standard dictionary and unknown words are flagged. You can then ignore the word, correct it, or add it to the dictionary.

To check spelling in a portion of a document, select the text to check. Otherwise, Word will check the entire document starting at the location of the cursor. If you want to check starting at the beginning of the document, move the insertion point to the start of the document by pressing Ctrl+Home. Then:

1. Select Tools, Spelling and Grammar; press F7; or click the Spelling and Grammar button on the Standard toolbar. The Spelling and Grammar dialog box appears (see Figure 21.1). If you want to check spelling only, deselect the Check Grammar check box. The remainder of these steps assume that you are checking spelling only. If not, Word will flag suspected grammar errors; how you deal with these is described later in this lesson.

2. When Word locates a word in the document that is not in the dictionary, it displays the word and its surrounding text in the Not In Dictionary box with the word high-lighted in red. In Figure 21.1, for example, the word **checker** is highlighted. Suggested replacements for the word appear in the Suggestions box (if Word has no sug-gestions, this box will be empty). Then:

- To correct the word manually, edit it in the Not In Dictionary box and select Change.

- To use one of the suggested replacements, highlight the desired replacement word in the Suggestions box and select Change.

- To replace all instances of the word in the document with either the manual corrections you made or the word selected in the Suggestions box, select Change All.

- To ignore this instance of the word, select Ignore.

- To ignore this and all other instances of the word in the document, select Ignore All.

- To add the word to the dictionary, select Add.

3. Repeat as needed. When the entire document has been checked, Word displays a message to that effect. Or, select Cancel to end spell checking early.

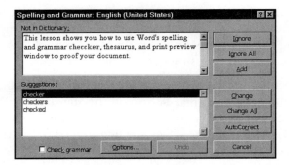

FIGURE 21.1 Checking spelling in the Spelling and Grammar dialog box.

Use AutoCorrect To add a misspelled word and its correction to the AutoCorrect list, select AutoCorrect in the Spelling and Grammar dialog box. Future misspellings will then be corrected automatically as you type them.

CHECKING YOUR GRAMMAR

Word can check the grammar of the text in your document, flagging possible problems so you can correct them if needed. Here are the steps required:

1. Select Tools, Spelling and Grammar; press F7; or click the Spelling and Grammar button on the toolbar. The Spelling and Grammar dialog box appears (refer to Figure 21.1). Make sure the Check Grammar check box is selected.

2. When Word locates a word or phrase with a suspected grammatical error, it displays the word or phrase and its surrounding text in the dialog box with the word highlighted in green and a description of the suspected problem above the text. In Figure 21.2, for example, the word **want** is highlighted and the problem **Subject-Verb Agreement** appears. Suggested fixes, if any, are listed in the Suggestions list box. Then:

   - To manually correct the error, edit the text then select Change.

   - To use one of the suggested replacements, select it in the Suggestions list box and select Change.

   - To ignore this instance of the problem, select Ignore.

   - To ignore this instance and all other instances of the problem in the document, select Ignore All.

3. Word will check spelling at the same time it is checking grammar. Deal with spelling errors as explained earlier in this lesson.

4. Repeat as needed. When the entire document has been checked, Word displays a message to that effect. Or, select Close to end grammar checking early.

TIP   **Don't Rely on Word**   Word's grammar checker is a useful tool, but don't rely on it to catch everything. It is no substitute for careful writing and editing.

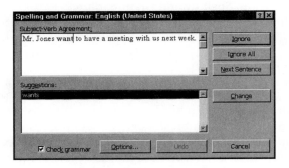

FIGURE 21.2   Checking grammar in the Spelling and Grammar dialog box.

CHECKING SPELLING AND GRAMMAR AS YOU TYPE

In addition to checking your document's spelling and grammar all at once, Word can check text as you type it. Words not found in the dictionary will be underlined with a wavy red line, and suspected grammatical errors will be marked with a wavy green line. You can deal with the errors immediately or whenever you choose. To turn automatic spell/grammar checking on or off:

1. Select Tools, Options to open the Options dialog box.

2. If necessary, click the Spelling and Grammar tab.

3. Select or deselect the Check Spelling as You Type and the Check Grammar as You Type check boxes.

4. Click OK.

To deal with a word that has been underlined by automatic spell or grammar checking, right-click the word. A pop-up menu appears, containing suggested replacements for the word (if any are found) as well as several commands. Figure 21.3 shows the pop-up menu that appears when you right-click a misspelled word. For a spelling error, your choices are:

- To replace the word with one of the suggestions, click the replacement word.

- To ignore all occurrences of the word in the document, click Ignore All.

- To add the word to the dictionary, click Add.

- To add the misspelling to the AutoCorrect list, select AutoCorrect then select the proper replacement spelling.

- To start a regular spelling check, click Spelling.

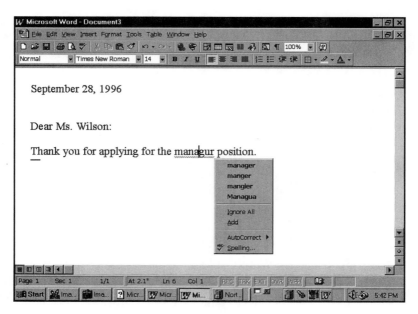

FIGURE 21.3   Correcting spelling as you type.

When you right-click a grammatical error, you are offered the following choices:

- Select a suggested replacement to insert it in the document.

- Select Ignore Sentence to ignore the possible error.

- Select Grammar to start a regular grammar check.

Hide Spelling/Grammar Marks   If your document contains words underlined by the automatic spelling or grammar checker and you want to hide the underlines, select Tools, Options, click the Spelling and Grammar tab, and select the Hide Spelling Errors in this Document check box or the Hide Grammatical Errors in this Document check box. Deselect these check boxes to redisplay the underlines.

Using the Thesaurus

A thesaurus provides you with synonyms and antonyms for words in your document. Using the thesaurus can help you avoid repetition in your writing (and improve your vocabulary).

Synonyms and Antonyms   Words with the same and opposite meanings, respectively, as a given word.

To use the thesaurus:

1. Place the insertion point on the word of interest in your document.

2. Press Shift+F7, or select Language, Tools, and Thesaurus.

3. The Thesaurus dialog box opens (see Figure 21.4). This dialog box has several components:

- The Looked Up box displays the word of interest.

- The Meanings box lists alternate meanings for the word. If the word is not found, Word displays an Alphabetical List box instead; this contains a list of words with spellings similar to the selected word.

- If the thesaurus finds one or more meanings for the word, the dialog box displays the Replace with Synonym list showing synonyms for the currently highlighted meaning of the word. If meanings are not found, the dialog box displays a Replace with Related Word list.

4. While the Thesaurus dialog box is displayed, there are several actions you can take:

- To find synonyms for the highlighted word in the Replace with Synonym list or the Replace with Related Words list (depending on which one is displayed), select Look Up.

- To find synonyms for a word in the Meanings list, select the word and then select Look Up.

- For some words, the thesaurus displays the term Antonyms in the Meanings list. To display antonyms for the selected word, highlight the term Antonyms and then select Look Up.

5. To replace the word in the document with the highlighted word in the Replace with Synonym list or the Replace with Related Word list, select Replace.

6. To close the thesaurus without making any changes to the document, select Cancel.

What Does it Mean?   You can use the thesaurus like a dictionary to find the meaning of words you are not familiar with.

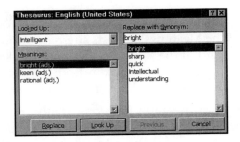

FIGURE 21.4   The Thesaurus dialog box.

USING PRINT PREVIEW

Word's Print Preview feature lets you view your document on the screen exactly as it will be printed. While Page Layout view also displays your document in its final form, Print Preview offers some additional features that you may find useful. To use Print Preview, select File, Print Preview or click the Print Preview button on the Standard toolbar. The current page appears in the Preview window (see Figure 21.5). Then:

- Press Page Up or Page Down, or use the scroll bar, to view other pages.

- Click the Multiple Pages button, then drag over the page icons to preview more than one page at once. Click the One Page button to preview a single page.

- Click the Zoom Control drop-down arrow and select a magnification to preview the document at different magnifications.

- Click the View Ruler button to display the Ruler. You can then use the Ruler to set page margins and indents as described in Lessons 10 and 14.

- Click the Magnifier button and click in the document to enlarge that part of the document.

- Click the Shrink to Fit button to prevent a small amount of text from spilling onto the document's last page. Word will attempt to adjust formatting to reduce the page count by one.

- Click the Print button to print the document. Click again to return to the original view.

- Click Close or press Esc to end Print Preview display.

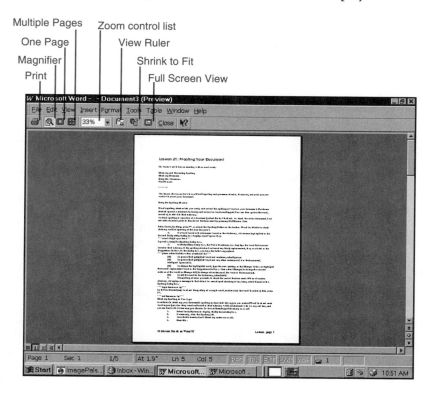

FIGURE 21.5   The Print Preview window.

In this lesson, you learned how to use Word's proofing tools to check your document's spelling and grammar, and how to use the thesaurus and Print Preview. The next lesson shows you how to use tables.

22 WORKING WITH TABLES

In this lesson, you learn how to add tables to your document, and how to edit and format tables.

WHAT'S A TABLE?

A *table* lets you organize information in a row and column format. Each entry in a table, called a *cell*, is independent of all other entries. You can have almost any number of rows and columns in a table. You also have a great deal of control over the size and formatting of each cell. A table cell can contain text, graphics, and just about anything that a Word document can contain. The one exception is that a table cannot contain another table.

TIP **On the Table** Use tables for columns of numbers, lists, and anything else that requires a row and column arrangement.

INSERTING A TABLE

To insert a new, empty table at any location within your document, follow these steps:

1. Move the cursor to the document location where you want the table.

2. Select Table, Insert Table. The Insert Table dialog box appears (see Figure 22.1).

3. In the Number of Columns and Number of Rows text boxes, click the arrows or enter the number of rows and

columns the table should have. (You can adjust these numbers later.)

4. To apply one of Word's automatic table formats to the table, click the AutoFormat button, select the desired format, then click OK. (AutoFormat is covered in more detail later in this lesson.)

5. In the Column Width text box, select the desired width for each column, in inches. Select Auto to have the page width evenly divided among the specified number of columns.

6. Select OK. A blank table is created with the cursor in the first cell.

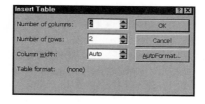

FIGURE 22.1 The Insert Table dialog box.

 Quick Tables To quickly insert a table, click the Insert Table button on the Standard toolbar, then drag over the desired number of rows and columns.

WORKING IN A TABLE

When the cursor is in a table cell, you can enter and edit text as you would in the rest of the document. Text entered in a cell automatically wraps to the next line within the column width. You can move the cursor to any cell by clicking it. You can also navigate in a table using the following special key combinations:

PRESS THIS	TO MOVE HERE
Tab	The next cell in a row
Shift+Tab	The previous cell in a row
Alt+Home	The first cell in the current row
Alt+Page Up	The top cell in the current column
Alt+End	The last cell in the current row
Alt+Page Down	The last cell in the current column

If the cursor is at the edge of a cell, you can use the arrow keys to move between cells. To insert a Tab in a table cell, press Ctrl+Tab.

EDITING AND FORMATTING A TABLE

After you create a table and enter some information, you can edit its contents and format its appearance to suit your needs.

DELETING AND INSERTING CELLS, ROWS, AND COLUMNS

You can clear individual cells in a table, erasing their contents and leaving a blank cell. You can also remove entire rows and columns. When you do so, columns to the right or rows below move to fill in for the deleted row or column.

TIP   **Fast Select!**   You can select the text in the cell or the entire cell itself. To select an entire cell, click in the left margin of the cell, between the text and the cell border. The mouse pointer changes to an arrow when it's in this area.

To clear the contents of a cell, select the cell and press Delete.

To remove an entire row or column from the table:

1. Move the cursor to any cell in the row or column to be deleted.

2. Select Table, Delete Cells. The Delete Cells dialog box appears (see Figure 22.2).

3. Select Delete Entire Row or Delete Entire Column.

4. Select OK. The row or column is deleted.

 Recovery Remember that you can undo table editing actions with the Edit, Undo command.

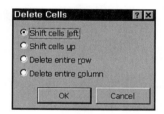

FIGURE 22.2 The Delete Cells dialog box.

To insert a single row or column into a table:

1. Move the cursor to a cell to the right of where you want the new column or below where you want the new row.

2. Select Table, Insert Columns to insert a new, blank column to the left of the selected column. Select Table, Insert Rows to insert a new, blank row above the selected row.

 Changing Commands? The commands on the Table menu change according to circumstances. For example, if you select a column in a table, the Insert Columns command is displayed but the Insert Rows command is not.

To insert more than one row or column into a table:

1. Select cells that span the number of rows or columns you want to insert. For example, to insert three new rows between rows 2 and 3, select cells in rows 3, 4, and 5 (in any column).

2. Select Table, Select Row (if inserting rows) or Table, Select Column (if inserting columns).

3. Select Table, Insert Rows or Table, Insert Columns, as appropriate.

 Add a Row   To insert a new row at the bottom of the table, move the cursor to the last cell in the table and press Tab.

To insert a new column at the right edge of the table:

1. Click just outside the table's right border.

2. Select Table, Select Column.

3. Select Table, Insert Columns.

MOVING OR COPYING COLUMNS AND ROWS

Here's how to copy or move an entire column or row from one location in a table to another:

1. Select the column or row by dragging over the cells or by clicking in the column or row then selecting Table, Select Row or Table, Select Column.

2. To copy, press Ctrl+C or click the Copy button on the Standard toolbar. To move, press Ctrl+X or click the Cut button.

3. Move the cursor to the new location for the column or row. It will be inserted above or to the left of the location of the cursor.

4. Press Ctrl+V or click the Paste button on the Standard toolbar.

CHANGING COLUMN WIDTH

You can quickly change the width of a column with the mouse:

1. Point at the right border of the column whose width you want to change. The mouse pointer changes to a pair of thin vertical lines with arrowheads pointing left and right.

2. Drag the column border to the desired width.

You can also use a dialog box to change column widths:

1. Move the cursor to any cell in the column you want to change.

2. Select Table, Cell Height and Width. The Cell Height and Width dialog box appears (see Figure 22.3). If necessary, click the Column tab to display the column options.

3. In the Width of Column text box, enter the desired column width, or click the incrementer arrows to change the setting. Note that the label identifies which column you are working on by number. To automatically adjust the column width to fit the widest cell entry, click the Autofit button.

4. Change the value in the Space Between Columns text box to modify spacing between columns. Changing this setting increases or decreases the amount of space between the text in each cell and the cell's left and right borders.

5. Click Next Column or Previous Column to change the settings for other columns in the table.

6. Select OK. The table changes to reflect the new column settings.

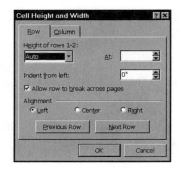

FIGURE 22.3   Changing column width.

TABLE BORDERS

Word's default is to place a single, thin border around each cell in a table. You can modify the borders, or remove them altogether. The techniques for working with table borders are essentially the same as for adding borders to other text (see Lesson 9). Briefly, here are the steps involved.

1. Select the table cells whose borders you want to modify.

2. Select Format, Borders and Shading to display the Borders and Shading dialog box. Click the Borders tab if necessary (refer to Figure 9.3).

3. Select the desired border settings, using the Preview box to see how your settings will appear.

4. Select OK.

In a table with no borders, you can display non-printing gridlines on-screen to make it easier to work with the table. Select Table, Show Gridline to display gridlines, and select Table, Hide Gridlines to turn them off.

AUTOMATIC TABLE FORMATTING

Word provides a variety of predefined table formats. Using these formats makes it easy to apply attractive formatting to any table:

1. Place the cursor anywhere in the table.

2. Select Table, Table AutoFormat. The Table AutoFormat dialog box appears (see Figure 22.4). This is the same dialog box you would see if you selected AutoFormat in the Insert Table dialog box when first creating a table, as covered earlier in this lesson.

3. Formats lists the available table formats. As you scroll through the list, the Preview box shows the appearance of the highlighted format.

4. Select and deselect the formatting check boxes as needed until the Preview shows the table appearance you want.

5. Select OK. The selected formatting is applied to the table.

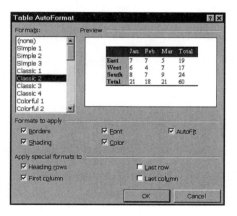

FIGURE 22.4 The Table AutoFormat dialog box.

In this lesson, you learned how to add tables to your document, and how to edit and format tables. The next lesson shows you how to use columns in your documents.

23 USING COLUMNS IN YOUR DOCUMENTS

In this lesson, you learn how to format your document text in two or more columns per page.

WHY USE COLUMNS?

Columns are commonly used in newsletters, brochures, and similar documents. The shorter lines of text provided by columns are easier to read, and they provide greater flexibility in formatting a document with graphics, tables, and so on. Word makes it easy to use columns in your documents. Figure 23.1 shows a document formatted with two columns.

The columns you create in Word are *newspaper* style columns, in which the text flows to the bottom of one column and then continues at the top of the next column on the page. For side-by-side paragraphs, such as you would need in a resume or a script, use Word's table feature, which is covered in Lesson 22.

When you define columns with text selected, the column definition will apply to the selected text. Word will insert section breaks before and after the selection. If you do not select text first, the column definitions will apply to the entire document unless you divided the document into two or more sections, in which case the columns will apply only to the current section. See Lesson 14 for more information about document sections.

Line between columns

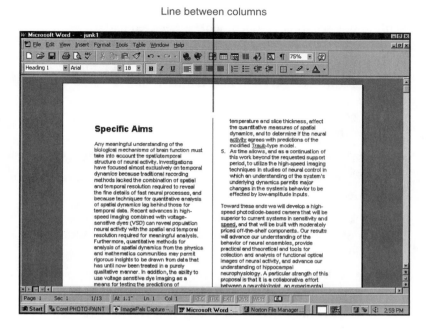

FIGURE 23.1   A document formatted with two columns.

CREATING COLUMNS

Word has four predefined column layouts:

- Two equal width columns

- Three equal width columns

- Two unequal width columns with the wider column on the left

- Two unequal width columns with the wider column on the right

You can apply any of these column formats to an entire document, to one section of a document, to selected text, or from the insertion point onward. Follow these steps:

1. If you want only a part of the document in columns, select the text you want in columns, or move the insertion point to the location where you want columns to begin. Word will insert section breaks before and/or after the text, as needed.

2. Select Format, Columns to open the Columns dialog box (see Figure 23.2).

3. Under Presets, click the column format you want.

4. Click the Apply To drop-down arrow and specify the extent to which the columns should apply. The following options are available:

   - **Whole Document** This is available only if the document has not been broken into sections.

   - **This Section** Available only if you have broken the document into sections.

   - **This Point Forward** Word will insert a section break at the current cursor location and apply the new column setting to the latter of the two sections.

5. Select the Line Between check box to display a vertical line between columns (like in a newspaper).

6. Select OK.

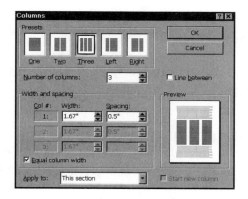

FIGURE 23.2   The Columns dialog box.

Quick Columns   To display selected text, the current section, or the entire document in one to four equal width columns, click the Columns button on the Standard toolbar, then drag over the desired number of columns.

No Columns?   Columns display on-screen only in Page Layout view. In Normal view, Word displays only a single column at a time (although your multiple columns will look fine when printed, even from Normal view). To switch to Page Layout view, select View, Page Layout.

MODIFYING COLUMNS

You can modify existing columns, change the number of columns, change column widths, and change the spacing between columns. Here's how:

1. Move the cursor to the columns you want to modify.

2. Select Format, Columns to open the Columns dialog box (refer to Figure 23.2). The options in the dialog box will reflect the current settings for the columns you selected.

3. To apply a different predefined column format, click the desired format in the Presets area of the dialog box.

4. To change the width or spacing of a specific column, enter the desired width and spacing values (or click the arrows) in the column's Width and Spacing text boxes. The Preview box shows you what the settings will look like.

5. Select OK.

Turning Columns Off

To convert multiple column text back to normal text (which is really just one column), follow these steps:

1. Select the text that you want to change from multiple columns to a single column.

2. Select Format, Columns to open the Columns dialog box (refer to Figure 23.2).

3. Under Presets, select the One option.

4. Select OK.

A Quicker Way   To quickly convert text in columns back to normal single-column text, select the text then click the Columns button on the Standard toolbar and drag to select a single column.

This lesson showed you how to arrange text in columns. The next lesson shows you how to work with graphics in your document.

ADDING GRAPHICS TO YOUR DOCUMENT

In this lesson, you learn how to add graphics to your documents, and how to create your own drawings.

ADDING A GRAPHIC IMAGE

A *graphic image* is a picture that is stored on disk in a graphics file. Word can utilize graphics files created by a variety of applications, including PC Paintbrush, Windows' own Paint program, Lotus 1-2-3, Micrografx Designer, and AutoCAD. Additionally, your Word installation includes a small library of clip art images that you can use in your documents. Figure 24.1 shows a document with a graphic image.

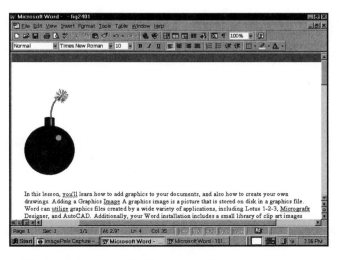

FIGURE 24.1 A document with a graphic.

To add a graphic image to a Word document, follow these steps:

1. Move the insertion point to the location for the graphic.

2. Select Insert, Picture, From File. The Insert Picture dialog box appears (see Figure 24.2).

3. If necessary, click the Look In drop-down arrow to specify the folder where the graphic file is located.

4. The large box in the center of the dialog box normally lists all graphics files in the specified directory. To have the list restricted to certain types of graphics files, click the Files of Type drop-down arrow and select the desired file type from the list.

5. In the File Name text box, type the name of the file to insert, or select the file name from the list.

6. To preview the picture in the Preview box, click the Preview button.

7. Select options as follows:

   - Select Link to File if you want the graphic in your document updated if the graphics file on disk changes. *Use on division addresses in letterhead*

   - If you selected Link to File, you can select Save with Document to save a copy of the picture with the document. Although this increases the document's file size, it permits the picture to be displayed even if the original file is no longer available.

   - Select Float Over Text *no* to enable the picture to be displayed "behind" or "over" text and other objects. Otherwise, the image will be displayed inline with text.

8. Select OK. The graphic is inserted into your document.

Preview button

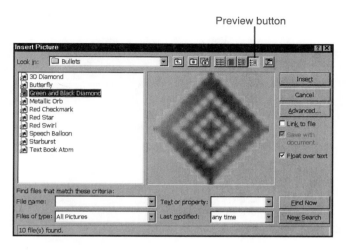

FIGURE 24.2   The Insert Picture dialog box.

ADDING CLIP ART

Clip art is a special category of pictures that consists of generally small, simple images that you can use to add visual appeal and interest to your documents. Word comes with an extensive gallery of clip art that you can use freely. Here's how to add a clip art image to a document:

1. Move the cursor to the document location where you want the image.

2. Select Insert, Picture, Clip Art to open the Microsoft Clip Gallery dialog box (see Figure 24.3).

3. In the list on the left, select the desired category of image. Or, select (**All Categories**) to view all clip art images.

4. Scroll through the image list until you find the image you want, then click it to select it.

5. Select Insert to add the image to your document.

Word on the Web   If you have Internet access, you can click the Connect to Web button in the Microsoft Clip Gallery dialog box to connect to Microsoft's Web site, where you can access additional clip art images.

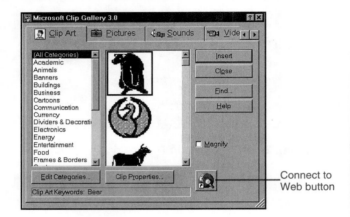

Connect to Web button

FIGURE 24.3   Selecting clip art from the Microsoft Clip Gallery.

DISPLAYING GRAPHICS

The screen display of graphics images can slow down screen scrolling. If you're working on the document text in Page Layout or Online Layout view and don't need to see the images, you can speed up screen display by displaying empty rectangles called *placeholders* in place of the images (images are automatically hidden in Normal and Outline view). In addition, if you selected the Link to File option when inserting the graphic file, Word inserts a field code in the document. The screen will display this code instead of the picture when field codes are displayed.

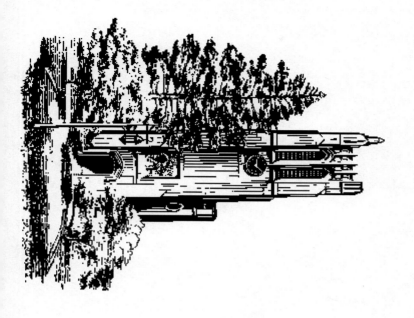

Example of a field code,
this is what prints. The document
shows "{INCLUDEPICTURE "\\\\HRNT2\\Letter
Head\\LTTOWER.TIF"*MERGEFORMAT\d}

Field Code   A code in a document that tells Word to display a certain item, such as a graphic.

Here's how to control the display of graphics:

1. Select Tools, Options to open the Options dialog box.

2. If necessary, click the View tab to display the View options.

3. In the Show section, select or deselect the Picture Placeholders and Field Codes check boxes as desired.

4. Select OK.

The screen display of placeholders or field codes does not affect printing, which will always include the actual graphics.

 TIP   **Speed it Up!**   When working on a document that contains a lot of graphics, you can speed up screen display and scrolling by displaying placeholders for the graphics.

CROPPING AND RESIZING A GRAPHIC

Before you can work with a graphic in your document, you must select it. There are two ways to do this:

• You can click the graphic with the mouse.

• With the keyboard, position the insertion point immediately to the left of the graphic, and press Shift+→.

A selected graphic is surrounded by eight small black squares called *sizing handles*, as shown in Figure 24.4.

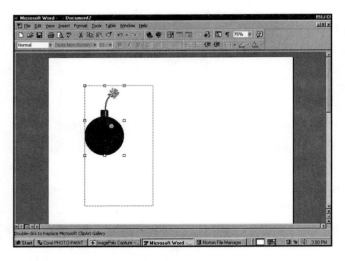

FIGURE 24.4   Resizing a selected graphic.

You can resize a graphic in your document, displaying the entire picture at a different size. You can also crop a graphic, hiding portions of the picture that you don't want to display. To resize or crop a graphic:

1. Select the graphic.

2. Point at one of the sizing handles. The mouse pointer will change to a double-headed arrow.

3. Do either or both of the following, depending on how you want to modify the image:

   - To resize the graphic, press the left mouse button and drag the handle until the outline of the graphic is at the desired size. You can either enlarge or shrink the graphic.

   - To crop the graphic, press and hold Shift, then press the left mouse button and drag a handle toward the center of the graphic.

4. Release the mouse button.

DELETING, MOVING, AND COPYING GRAPHICS

To delete a graphic, select it and press Delete. To move or copy a graphic to a new location:

1. Select the graphic.

2. To copy the graphic, press Ctrl+C; select Edit, Copy; or click the Copy button on the Standard toolbar. To move the graphic, press Ctrl+X; select Edit, Cut; or click the Cut button on the Standard toolbar.

3. Move the cursor to the new location for the graphic.

4. Press Ctrl+V; select Edit, Paste; or click the Paste button on the Standard toolbar.

> **TIP**   **Drag that Image**   If the image and its destination are both in view, you can move it by dragging it to the new location. To copy instead of moving, hold down Ctrl while dragging.

DRAWING IN YOUR DOCUMENT

In addition to adding existing graphics to a document, Word lets you create your own drawings. The drawing tools that are available let even the complete non-artist create professional-looking drawings. To draw, you must display the Drawing toolbar. Select View, Toolbars, Drawing. Figure 24.5 shows the Drawing toolbar, and identifies its buttons.

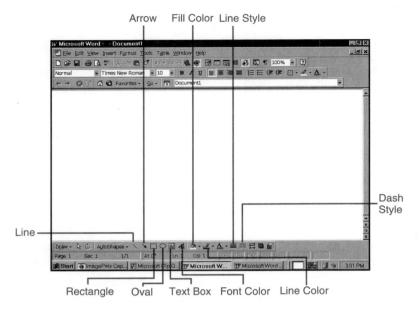

FIGURE 24.5   The Drawing toolbar.

The process of drawing consists of the following general actions:

- Adding drawing objects to the document. The available objects include lines, arrows, shapes, and text. Most of Word's drawing objects are called *AutoShapes*.

- Moving drawing objects to new locations and changing their size and proportions.

- Modifying drawing objects. For example, you might change the thickness of a line, the color of text, or the type of arrowhead on an arrow.

The Drawing toolbar displays buttons for the most commonly needed drawing objects: lines, arrows, 3D shapes, and so on. You access the less commonly needed drawing objects via menus or dialog boxes associated with the Drawing toolbar. The following list explains the most frequently used drawing procedures.

- To draw an object, click its button on the Drawing toolbar. Or, click the AutoShapes button and select the shape from the list. Then draw in the document to insert the object. Hold down Shift while drawing to draw an object with a 1:1 aspect ratio (for example, a square or circle instead of a rectangle or ellipse).

- To select an object you have already drawn, click it. The object will display sizing handles. Hold down Shift while clicking to select more than one object. Press Delete to delete the selected object(s).

- To move a selected object, point at it (but not at a handle) and drag to the new location.

- To change a selected object's size or shape, point at one of its resizing handles and drag to the desired size/shape.

- To change the color of an object's line, click the Line Color button on the Drawing toolbar and select the desired color.

- To change the interior color of a solid object, click the Fill Color button and select the desired color.

- To change the thickness or style of the lines used for an object, select the object then click the Line Style or Dash Style button.

- To add a text label, click the Text Box button, drag in the document to add the text box, then type the text. Click outside the text box when done.

Word's drawing capabilities go much further than what is described here. You should experiment on your own to discover their full capabilities.

In this lesson, you learned how to add graphics and drawings to your documents. The next lesson teaches you how to work with multiple documents.

WORKING WITH MULTIPLE DOCUMENTS

This lesson shows you how to simultaneously edit multiple documents in Word.

MULTIPLE DOCUMENTS?

Working on one document at a time is often all you need, but in some situations the capability to work on multiple documents at once can be very useful. For example, you can refer to one document while working on another, and you can copy and move text between documents. Word lets you have as many documents as you need open simultaneously.

STARTING OR OPENING A SECOND DOCUMENT

While you're working on one document, you can start a new document or open another existing document at any time. To do so, follow the procedures you learned in Lesson 2 for creating a new document and in Lesson 4 for opening a document. Briefly:

- To create a new document based on the Normal template, click the New button on the Standard toolbar.

- To create a document based on another template or one of Word's Wizards, select File, New.

- To open an existing document, select File, Open or click the Open button on the Standard toolbar.

A new window opens and displays the document you created or opened. Both the newly created and the original documents are in memory, and can be edited, printed, and so on. You can continue opening additional documents until all of the files you need to work with are open.

TIP   **Opening Multiple Documents at Once**   In the Open dialog box, you can select multiple documents by holding Shift while clicking the document names. Then select Open to open all of the selected documents.

SWITCHING BETWEEN DOCUMENTS

When you have multiple documents open at one time, only one of them can be *active* at a given moment. The active document is displayed on-screen (although inactive documents may be displayed as well). The title bar of the active document is displayed in a darker color, and if documents are overlapping each other, the active one will be on top. More important, the active document is the only one affected by editing commands.

To switch between open documents:

1. Select the Window menu. At the bottom is a list of all open documents with a check mark next to the name of the currently active document (see Figure 25.1).

2. Select the name of the document you want active. You can click the document name with the mouse or press the corresponding number key.

The selected document becomes active and appears on-screen.

TIP   **Next Please!**   To cycle to the next open document, press Ctrl+F6.

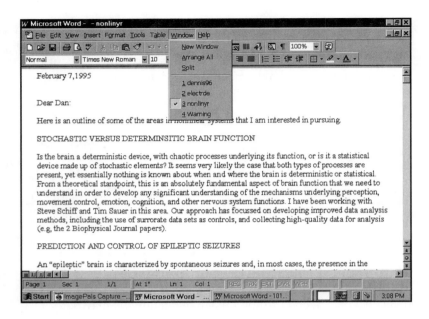

FIGURE 25.1   The Window menu lists open documents and indicates the currently active document.

CONTROLLING MULTIPLE DOCUMENT VIEW

Word gives you a great deal of flexibility in displaying multiple documents. You can have the active document occupy the entire screen, with other open documents temporarily hidden. You can also have several documents displayed at the same time, each in its own window. A document window can be in one of three states:

- **Maximized** The window occupies the entire work area and no other open documents are visible. When the active document is maximized, its title appears in Word's title bar at the top of the screen. Figure 25.2 shows a maximized document.

- **Minimized** The window is reduced to a small icon displayed at the bottom of the Word screen. The document title is displayed on the icon.

- **Restored** The document window assumes an intermediate size, and the document title is displayed in the title bar of its own window instead of Word's title bar.

Figure 25.3 shows both a restored and a minimized document.

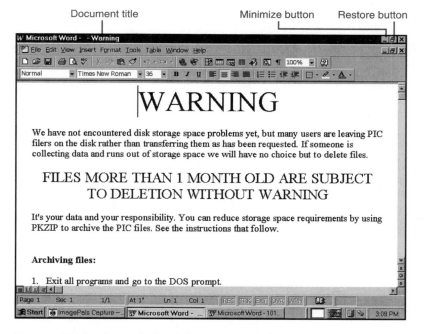

FIGURE 25.2   A maximized document window.

You can control the display of multiple documents as follows:

- To restore or minimize a maximized window, click its Restore or Minimize button.

- To maximize or minimize a restored window, click its Maximize or Minimize button.

- To display a minimized window, click its icon. Then, either click its Restore or Maximize button or select from the pop-up menu that appears.

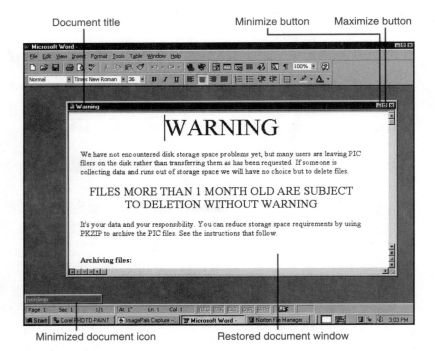

FIGURE 25.3   Restored and minimized document windows.

When a document is in the restored state, you can control the size and position of its window. To move the window, click its title bar and drag it to the new position. To change window size, point at a border or corner of the window (the mouse pointer changes to a two-headed arrow), then click and drag the window to the desired size.

Viewing All Open Documents

Word has a command that displays all of your open documents. Select Window, Arrange All to tile all document windows. When you tile your documents, every open document is displayed in a small window with no overlapping of windows. If you have more than a few documents open, these windows will be quite small and won't be very useful for editing. They are useful, however, for seeing exactly what documents you have open and finding the one you need to work on at the moment. Figure 25.4 shows the result of the Window, Arrange All command with four documents open.

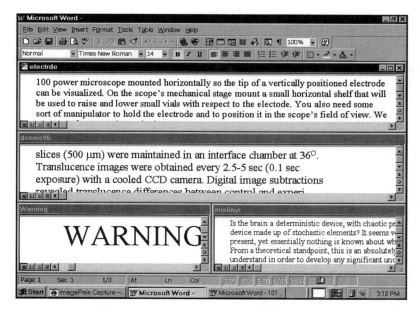

Figure 25.4 The Arrange All command displays all open documents, each in its own window.

MOVING AND COPYING TEXT BETWEEN DOCUMENTS

When you have more than one document open, you can move and copy text and graphics between documents. Follow these procedures:

1. Make the source document active, and select the text and/or graphic that is to be moved or copied.

2. Press Ctrl+X; select Edit, Cut; or click the Cut button on the Standard toolbar if you want to move the text. Press Ctrl+C; select Edit, Copy; or click the Copy button on the Standard toolbar to copy the text.

3. Make the destination document active. Move the insertion point to the location for the text.

4. Press Ctrl+V; select Edit, Paste; or click the Paste button on the Standard toolbar.

If both documents are visible, you can copy or move text from one to the other with drag-and-drop:

1. Select the text to be copied or moved.

2. Point at the selected text with the mouse. To move the text, press and hold the left mouse button. To copy the text, press Ctrl+left mouse button.

3. Drag to the new location for the text, and release the mouse button (and the Ctrl key, if you were copying).

SAVING MULTIPLE DOCUMENTS

When you're working with multiple documents, you save individual documents with the File, Save and File, Save As commands you learned about in Lesson 4. These commands save the active document only. There is no command to save all open documents in one step. If you attempt to close a document that has not been saved, you will be prompted to save it. If you try to quit Word with one or more unsaved documents, you will be prompted one-by-one to save each document.

 TIP **No Save All** The Save All command that was available in earlier versions of Word is no longer present in Word 97.

CLOSING A DOCUMENT

You can close an open document when you finish working with it. To close a document:

1. Make the document active.

2. Select File, Close or click the Close button at the right end of the document's title bar. Be sure not to click the Close button in Word's main title bar.

3. If the document contains unsaved changes, Word prompts you to save the document.

The document is closed.

This lesson showed you how to simultaneously edit multiple documents in Word. In the next lesson, you will learn how to use Word with the Word Wide Web.

26

WORD AND THE WORLD WIDE WEB

In this lesson, you learn you how to use Word in conjunction with the World Wide Web.

WHAT IS THE WEB?

The World Wide Web, or Web for short, is part of the Internet, a world-wide network that lets computer users share information and resources. The Web uses a specific document format called *hypertext markup language* (HTML) for its information. The Web also uses a type of address called a *uniform resource locator*, or URL, to identify specific documents and locations. Word offers a number of capabilities to help you work with HTML documents and URLs.

> **TIP** **HTML** Acronym for hypertext markup language, the document format used on the Web.

CREATING A WEB DOCUMENT

You can save any Word document in HTML format, which permits it to be used on the Web. You create and edit the document using the usual Word techniques, arranging text and graphics to appear on-screen as you want. When you save the document as an HTML file, Word converts the formatting in the document to the HTML codes required to reproduce the same or a similar appearance. However, not all Word formatting can be converted to HTML codes. This means that the final HTML document may not look exactly like the original Word document.

To save a Word document as an HTML file:

1. Select File, Save As to open the Save As dialog box.

2. Click the Save as Type drop-down arrow and select HTML Document from the list.

3. Enter the file name in the File Name text box.

4. Select OK.

EDITING A WEB DOCUMENT

You can use Word to edit existing Web documents in HTML format. When you open an HTML document, it is converted into Word format. When you save it, the document is converted back to HTML format. To open an HTML document for editing:

1. Select File, Open or click the Open button on the Standard toolbar to display the Open dialog box.

2. Click the Files of Type drop-down arrow and select HTML Document from the list.

3. Select the desired file in the Files list.

4. Select OK. The document will be displayed for editing.

5. Use Word's regular editing commands to make changes to the document.

6. Select File, Save or click the Save button on the Standard toolbar. The document will automatically be saved in HTML format.

WORKING WITH LINKS

A *link* is an address or pointer to something on the Web, such as a Web page or a person's e-mail address. The two types of links you will encounter most often are:

• A mail to link specifying an individual's e-mail address. For example, jsmith@abc.com.

- A hypertext link identifying a Web document. For example, http://www.abc.com.

Word has the capability to recognize links in a document and to treat them as links rather than as plain text. A link is actually a special case of document fields, which are covered in detail in Lesson 31. Links differ from plain text as follows:

- The link will be displayed in a special color and/or underlined.

- When you point at the link with your mouse, the mouse pointer will change to a pointing hand.

- You can delete the entire link but you cannot directly edit it.

- When you click a hypertext link, your Web browser will automatically start and display the Web page the link points to.

- When you click a mail to link, your e-mail program will automatically start and display a blank message already addressed to the address in the link.

The automatic activation of your Web browser and e-mail program is, of course, dependent on these programs being installed on your system. You can have Word automatically detect text that represents links as you type:

1. Select Tools, AutoCorrect to open the AutoCorrect dialog box.

2. If necessary, click the AutoFormat As You Type tab.

3. Select the Internet and Network Paths With Hyperlinks check box.

4. Select OK.

Another approach is to have Word go through existing text locating link text and converting it. This is part of the AutoFormat process, which was covered in detail in Lesson 16. Briefly, here are the required steps if you want to convert links and nothing else.

1. Select Format, AutoFormat to open the AutoFormat dialog box.

2. Select the AutoFormat Now check box.

3. Click the Options button to display the AutoFormat tab of the AutoCorrect dialog box, as shown in Figure 26.1.

4. Select the Internet and Network Paths with Hyperlinks check box.

5. Deselect all the other check boxes.

6. Select OK to return to the AutoFormat dialog box.

7. Click OK.

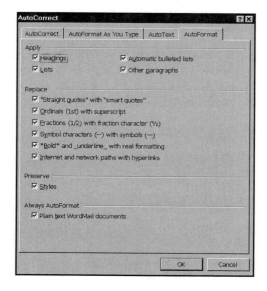

FIGURE 26.1 Setting AutoFormat options.

To convert a link back to regular text:

1. Position the cursor anywhere in the link. You'll have to use the keyboard to do this because clicking the link will activate it.

2. Press Ctrl+Shift+F9.

INSERTING A LINK

If you're working on a document, you can insert a link by simply typing its address and letting Word automatically identify it, as previously described. An easier way is to use the Insert, Hyperlink command. You can link to Internet files, Word documents, and various other types of files:

1. Select Insert, Hyperlink; press Ctrl+K; or click the Insert Hyperlink button on the Standard toolbar. The Insert Hyperlink dialog box appears (see Figure 26.2).

2. If you know the link address, type it in the Link to File or URL text box. To locate a file on your disk or your local network, click the Browse button and use the Link to File dialog box to locate the file.

3. If you want to link to a specific location in the file (such as a bookmark in a Word document), enter the name in the Named Location in File text box. Or, click the Browse button to select from a list of locations that are available in the file you selected in step 2.

4. Select OK.

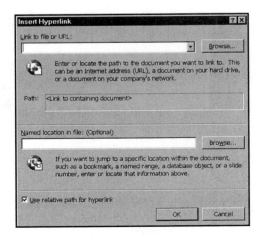

FIGURE 26.2   Adding a link to a document.

TIP

Use the Web Toolbar   Word's Web toolbar provides quick access to many Internet-related commands. To display it, select View, Toolbars, Web or click the Web Toolbar button on the Standard toolbar.

In this lesson, you learned how to use Word's Web-related features. The next lesson shows you how to save time by using macros.

27 REVISION MARKS AND MULTIPLE VERSIONS

In this lesson, you learn how to use Word's revision and version capabilities.

WHY USE REVISIONS?

Word's revision features are very useful when more than one person is working on a document. For example, an author can send a document to an editor, who enters suggested changes to text and formatting. With revision marks, both the original text and the suggested changes will be present in the document. When the document is returned to the author, he or she can review the suggested changes and either accept or reject them. When a document is reviewed by more than one person, each reviewer's suggested changes can be uniquely identified by the text color.

TRACKING AND HIGHLIGHTING DOCUMENT CHANGES

Keeping track of changes and highlighting them in the document are two independent processes. There are three ways this can work:

- If you track changes without highlighting them, Word will keep track of document changes but not display revision marks on the screen. You can later turn on revision mark display to show the previous changes.

- If you highlight changes without tracking them, earlier document changes that were made when tracking was turned on will be highlighted, but new changes will not be tracked or marked.

- If you both track and highlight changes, Word will track new changes and mark both old and new ones. You will probably use this setting most often.

To control the tracking and marking of changes in a document:

1. Select Tools, Track Changes, Highlight Changes. The Highlight Changes dialog box appears (see Figure 27.1).

2. Select or deselect the Track Changes While Editing and the Highlight Changes on Screen check boxes as desired. If you also want the changes highlighted when the document is printed, select the Highlight Changes in Printed Document check box.

3. Select OK.

FIGURE 27.1   The Highlight Changes dialog box.

TIP   **Fast Track**   To quickly turn tracking of document changes on or off, double-click the TRK indicator in Word's status bar. This toggles the Track Changes While Editing check box on or off.

Revision marks are displayed as follows:

- Changed text is displayed in a different color and with a vertical line in the outside margin; the color of the text identifies the reviewer who made the changes. If multiple individuals have revised the document, each person's revisions are displayed in a different color (with a maximum of eight reviewers).

- Newly added text is displayed with an underline.

- Deleted text is displayed with strikethrough, ~~like this~~, and in a text color that identifies the reviewer who made the deletion.

SETTING REVISION MARK OPTIONS

Word lets you control the way that revised text is marked. To set these options:

1. Select Tools, Track Changes, Highlight Changes to open the Highlight Changes dialog box (refer to Figure 27.1).

2. Click the Options button to open the Track Changes dialog box (see Figure 27.2).

3. There are four ways Word can mark changes: with inserted text, deleted text, changed formatting, or changed lines. To specify the type of mark used for each type of change, click the Mark drop-down arrow in the corresponding section of the dialog box and select the mark from the list. Select (**none**) if you do not want this type of change marked.

4. For each type of change, click the Color drop-down arrow and select the color to be used from the list. If you select By Author, Word will automatically assign a different color to each of as many as eight reviewers. If you select a specific color, all changes will be marked with that color regardless of who made them.

5. Select OK.

Who am I? Word identifies document reviewers by the user information you enter. This information is used by all Microsoft Office applications, not just Word. Select Tools, Options and click the User Information tab to view or change your user information.

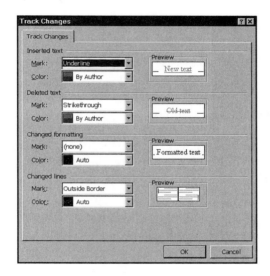

FIGURE 27.2 Specifying how Word marks document changes in the Track Changes dialog box.

 Use Comments Too Some reviewers prefer to include suggestions in the document as comments. The use of comments was covered in Lesson 28.

ACCEPTING OR REJECTING CHANGES

After a document has been reviewed by one or more reviewers, you will need to go through the text and either accept or reject the suggested changes. When you accept changes:

- Text identified as **Inserted** is made part of the document.

- Text identified as **Deleted** is permanently deleted.

- Formatting changes are permanently applied.

- Revision marks are removed.

When you reject changes:

- Text identified as **Inserted** is removed.

- Text identified as **Deleted** is restored.

- Formatting changes are reversed.

- Revision marks are removed.

You can accept or reject all changes in one step, or you can browse through the document, viewing individual changes and accepting or rejecting them one at a time. Here are the steps to follow:

1. Move the cursor to the document location where you want to start reviewing changes.

2. Select Tools, Track Changes, Accept or Reject Changes. The Accept or Reject Changes dialog box appears, as shown in Figure 27.3.

3. You can click in the document and scroll around while keeping the dialog box displayed. In the View area, select how you want the document displayed:

   - **Changes with Highlighting** Displays both the changes and the revision marks.

   - **Changes without Highlighting** Displays the changes but not the revision marks.

   - **Original** Hides both the changes and the revision marks.

4. Select Accept All or Reject All to accept or reject all changes in the document.

5. To review individual changes, click ←Find or →Find to move to the previous or next change in the document. Word will highlight the change and display information about the identity of the reviewer, the change made (for example, Inserted or Deleted), and the date and time of the change in the Changes area of the dialog box. You can then click Accept or Reject to accept or reject the change.

6. Click Undo to reverse the most recent acceptance or rejection.

7. When you are finished, select Close.

FIGURE 27.3   Accepting or rejecting document changes.

USING DOCUMENT VERSIONS

Sometimes you may want to save different versions of a document as you work on it. One way to do this is to use Word's File, Save As command to save each version of the document under a different file name. The File, Versions command, new to this release of Word, lets you keep different versions of a document together in a single file, making them easier to keep track of and saving disk space too.

To save the current document version:

1. Select File, Versions to open the Versions dialog box (see Figure 27.4).

2. Click the Save Now button.

3. Enter any comments to identify the current version. The date and time will automatically be included.

4. Select OK.

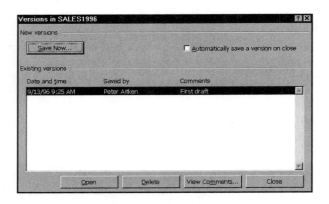

Figure 27.4   The Versions dialog box.

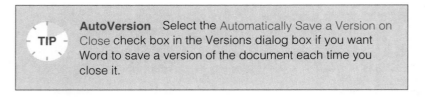

TIP   **AutoVersion** Select the Automatically Save a Version on Close check box in the Versions dialog box if you want Word to save a version of the document each time you close it.

To view or delete a specific version of the current document:

1. Select File, Versions to open the Versions dialog box (refer to Figure 27.4).

2. Select the desired version from the Existing Versions list, which displays all versions of the document.

3. Click Open to display the version, or click Delete to delete the version.

When you display an earlier version of a document, you can view and print it but you cannot edit it. If you want to modify a previous version, you must first save it as a separate document with the File, Save As command.

This lesson showed you how to use Word's revision and version capabilities. In the next lesson, you will learn how to work with mail merge.

INDEX